Move from Employee to CEO of Your Own Destiny

To order additional copies, please contact us.
BookSurge, LLC
www.booksurge.com
1-866-308-6235
orders@booksurge.com

MARY-ANN
MASSAD JOHNSON

MOVE FROM EMPLOYEE TO CEO OF YOUR OWN DESTINY

A Woman's Guide to Entrepreneurship and Wealth

2005

Move from Employee to CEO of Your Own Destiny

TABLE OF CONTENTS

This Book Is Dedicated To Palle, Nicholas, And Gregory, My Three Caballeros…….. You Have Inspired Me To Reach Beyond My Limits.

PREFACE AND ACKNOWLEDGEMENTS

I have been working in the information technology industry for over 21 years and have been blessed with a wonderful career. About ten years ago, I decided to take everything I knew about my industry and launch my own company, a strategic information technology management consulting firm called Knowsys Group.

Knowsys is derived from the Greek word, gnosis, meaning knowledge and wisdom. I anglicized the word to make it relevant to the information technology industry. I chose this meaning for our company, because I believed and still do, that the value we bring to our clients is the knowledge and wisdom to solve very complex business and technology challenges.

Knowsys Group has been the source of my greatest achievements over these last ten years. It allowed me to begin to actualize the potential I had glimpsed in myself, while I was working for other people.

Over the last year, I began to ponder what I would do with my life and the company as I move into my second act-the next forty years. Of course, growing our company is an important goal for me to achieve. But I began to think long and hard about how I wanted to grow our company. What do I want to do for the next forty years of life? What do I want to achieve? How will I grow as a human being and a business woman?

The seeds of this book and my motivational speaking series began to take shape in my mind, inspired by messages coming at me from many different sources. I have always loved to read and listen to motivational authors. As I drive to meetings with customers, I usually listen to an interesting motivational tape that keeps me company through hours of traffic and driving, and keeps my mind engaged.

The more I listened to these tapes, the more I realized that I shared many similar experiences, attitudes, and values with the authors.

Then, one day back in July of 2005, I got a call from my banker, Terryl Burrows, telling me that the Royal Bank of Canada was nominating me for an award called "Woman Entrepreneur of the Year". As I prepared the submission which the judges would read to determine if I was a winner, I began to really take stock of what I had accomplished over the years.

Through my initiation, creativity, and by trusting my instincts, Knowsys Group was launched in May of 1995. By 1998, and at the age of 35, I became a self-made millionaire. Our wealth and achievements have steadily grown through good and bad times. In observing this constant momentum of achievement, I began to realize that I might have some valuable knowledge to share with others.

On my way to tango class one Monday night with my cousin Demetra, she began telling me about some of the motivational speakers invited to speak at Dental Professional Development Seminars for her own company, ADL Dental Labs. The light bulb went off in my head at that moment. I realized that I could transform myself into a motivational speaker by leveraging my knowledge of building a multi-million dollar business.

This idea began to germinate in my head as my family and I headed to New York City for Thanksgiving. I began to speak at length to my husband about my idea to start a motivational speaking/education business.

As I jotted down notes for the course, seated in a comfortable chair in a Sean Jean Boutique on 5th Avenue, waiting for my sons to try on clothing, I realized that these notes could be used as the basis for a book, in addition to the crash course I was preparing for potential entrepreneurs.

By the end of our weekend in New York, I had drafted the outline to a course and book geared to helping women become successful entrepreneurs.

I decided to focus on helping women entrepreneurs for many reasons. Empowering women has always been a big part of who I am and how I interact with other women. I have observed that women in general do not appreciate their own potential or strengths. Just eavesdrop on a typical conversation between two women, and you will notice that, by and large, women are overly critical of themselves and are reluctant to toot their own horns.

I also looked around the world and observed from talking to people, traveling, and reading, that economics can either empower or enslave women. Certainly being employed in a great job is a significant achievement and contributor to women being able to control their financial destiny. But for a woman, owning her own business can create financial freedom and power of an almost exponential order of magnitude.

I recently read an article discussing women entrepreneurs and why they start businesses. The writer was quoting some surveys and studies that a major bank had done about women entrepreneurs. The surveys said that women start businesses to create flexibility in their work-life balance, not to necessarily become wealthy.

The premise of this book is that you can do both. I did. You can become a self-made millionaire and achieve balance and flexibility in your life. I want to teach women how they can achieve both prosperity and have more time and energy for family or personal interests.

The exponential freedom that comes with the power to choose one's own destiny was what inspired the title of this book, *Move from Employee to CEO of Your Own Destiny*.

During the process of transformation a woman goes through—from being an employee to an entrepreneur—there are several deeper changes that occur in a woman's psyche. From my own experience, the financial transformation was simply the first and most superficial stage of my metamorphosis. The most critical change I went through was finally realizing that I had the power to create my own reality and that my financial security resided within myself.

When I finally understood that I had the power to create my own reality, it gave me tremendous confidence and faith in myself, but it also created a significant sense of responsibility as well. I began to realize that I could do anything I wanted to, but that my decisions affect everyone around me-my family, employees, and customers.

Therefore, by taking excellent care of myself-my physical and mental health-and maximizing joyful experiences, I actually deliver more value to everyone my life and business touches.

This fundamental value of honoring thyself first is alien and uncomfortable for most women—especially for me. I grew up in a household and with an extended family where all the women in the family put their needs last—to their emotional, spiritual, and physical detriment.

When I began to understand the magnitude of my own personal power, I finally learned the lesson of how to be good to myself first. By doing this consistently, I am better able to give of myself and perform my best. As soon as I start to slip-up and revert back to the old behaviors of trying to please everyone except myself, everything gets messed up, and I start to see this manifested in negative outcomes that touch every aspect of my life.

Abundance is available to each of us. Part of my journey of becoming CEO of my own destiny was to understand that if I did what I love and if it is compatible with who I am, a limitless source of abundance in all of its forms is available to me.

I want to provide women with the knowledge, wisdom, and tools to create an abundant and joyful life, rooted in the freedom to make their own choices. Helping women to start a business or grow their current business, whether it is a retail store or a high-tech firm is the goal of my book and seminar series.

This book is dedicated to the memory of my grandmother Filia, her sister Anna, and her only living sister Demetra, who were great entrepreneurs who owned a very successful fashion design house over fifty years ago in Cairo, Egypt. After my relatives left Egypt in 1963, my grandmother re-started her design and dress-making business at the age of fifty in Canada. My great aunts also re-started their respective businesses in Athens, Greece. My grandmother and her sisters were able to single-handedly support their respective families at critical junctions—where their husbands had lost their jobs either to economics, immigration, or illness.

Their courage, determination, shrewd business sense, and hard work are their legacy to me.

My husband, Palle, has been a great source of inspiration and support throughout the whole process of inception, growth, and transformation of Knowsys Group. He is officially responsible for keeping me humble and being brutally honest about the viability of anything that I pursue.

My mother, Elsie, waged and won her personal war against breast cancer this year. Watching her and supporting her through many battles, I began to understand where I got my talent for perseverance. It is to her that I owe my greatest thanks. She passed on the entrepreneurial genes in spades, and with them, unbeatable optimism. Optimism is the secret weapon of all great entrepreneurs.

INTRODUCTION

One of the most significant sources of economic growth today is the success of the small and medium-sized business sectors. The number of women entrepreneurs is growing faster than that of their male counterparts. Over 40% of small businesses in Canada are owned by women. According to the U.S. Center for Women's Business research, the number of women-owned businesses in the U.S. grew at twice the rate of all firms between 1997 and 2002. The U.S. Small Business Administration finds that women-owned businesses account for 28% of all privately-owned businesses and they employ 9.2 million people. They contribute $2.38 trillion in revenue to the U.S. economy.

On the other side of these statistics, there is a less positive story to be told. For example, the U.S. Small Business Administration found that 87% of women-owned businesses had receipts of less than $50,000. The 13% that produced more than $50,000 per year accounted for two-thirds of the receipts from women-owned sole proprietorships. Only 2.7% of women-owned sole proprietorships produced $200,000 or more annually.

There has never been a better time to for women to become entrepreneurs. Women and small business have had a positive impact on our economy and society. Yet women have not actualized their true money-making potential according to some of the statistics quoted earlier.

Making the Move from Employee to CEO of Your Own Destiny is a book focused on women either looking to start their own business or for those that have started a business but are looking to grow that business dramatically. This book is intended to teach women the knowledge and best practices to allow them to become self-made millionaires.

For many of you, exploring and tackling the entrepreneurship path is a very real option. You may be fed-up with the corporate rat-race, have lost your job in down-sizing, want to spend more quality time with your children, or have retired from your first career and are looking for another source of income and intellectual challenge.

I became a small business owner in 1995 and had the opportunity and the benefit of creating financial success, new jobs, and power over my destiny in so many ways.

My goal is to transfer my knowledge of starting and building a business to other women, so that they can experience the power and balance of entrepreneurship.

This book is divided into three sections: the preparation, execution, and reaping the benefits cycles.

The preparation cycle is devoted to all of the mental and physical groundwork required to give birth to your business. It is focused upon the budding entrepreneur who is at stage O—the idea stage. Chapters 1 through 5 will provide you with the discipline and steps required to get a viable business off the ground.

The execution cycle encompasses Chapters 6 through 11 and addresses every aspect of setting-up a business and getting it into the position of making money and fulfilling your mission.

The Reaping the Benefits cycle covers Chapters 12 through 16. This section is intended for those entrepreneurs who have been in business for a while and are now at the point where they want to see dramatic changes. These dramatic changes could involve the sizeable growth of your business, the passing on of your business to family members, selling the business, or perhaps even scaling down the business, such that you still derive income and pleasure from working in something that has become your passion-but you balance this working "passion" with other interests such as hobbies, education, or family interests.

This book is focused upon the ideas, attitudes, actions, and knowledge required to take you from concept to implementation of owning and operating a profitable business and becoming self-empowered in every aspect of your life. *Making the Move from Employee to CEO of Your Own Destiny* is just as much about manifesting your dreams, physically, as it is about the profound mental and spiritual transformation that you will experience as you make your way down this path.

PART 1
The Preparation Cycle

CHAPTER 1
Recognizing the Signs-Is it Time to Start Your Own Business?

Some people fantasize about having their own business from the time they are adolescents, and some people are ambivalent right up until the time that life forces their hand in that direction.

For myself, I started fantasizing about starting a business—any business—from the first month that I began working as a Systems Marketing Assistant, an entry-level professional position at Burroughs in 1985. I would go out for lunch with one of the colleagues that I had be-friended and talk endlessly about different ideas we had to start a business, a store, or a restaurant, or maybe even a technology company.

I continued this habit for the next ten years, which is how long it took me to mentally prepare for actually taking the plunge and starting my own business.

There were two specific events that are crystallized in my memory as being the moments when my idle fantasies became burning desire and hunger for the personal freedom that being an entrepreneur would bring me.

The first event happened about two years before I officially started my company. I was working for a large systems integration firm and was out-performing most of my colleagues except for one. In my first nine months with the company, I had generated close to $2.5 Million in new revenue and had landed a $20 MM systems integration contract that would allow my employer to take in an additional $5 MM in revenue over the following twelve months. On top of my great revenue numbers, all of my business ventures were extremely profitable with over 50% gross margin and close to 20% net profit after all expenses.

By any company's standards, I was a top performer. Not only did I know how to bring revenue in, I was also able to manage the projects and people to earn tremendous profit.

At the time, my employer was losing money on all of their projects with the exception of mine and one other colleague. At one point, the Senior Vice-President grudgingly pointed out that my business unit's profits and that of my other colleague were actually neutralizing all the losses.

When my performance appraisal came due, I made my case to my immediate Vice-President and his boss, the Regional Vice-President, that I had outperformed 90% of the staff to date and had created profitable and high-profile business opportunities for the firm. Do you know what their response was? They agreed that I had done a wonderful job and should receive some kind of raise-a token of their appreciation. When I voiced my belief and argument that I should be promoted to Vice-President, their response, in not so many words, was that I was not VP-material. For my contribution of over $8-10 MM in my first twelve months of employment, they would grant me a paltry $10,000 bonus-which after tax would net me $5,000.

Do you want to know what my response to this let-down was? I developed a depression so deep that I had to take a month of medical leave to get out of my funk. A month later and feeling better on an anti-depressant, I came back to work and promptly requested a transfer to another office.

This experience created a heat in my soul to escape employment in a large corporation, which I was beginning to perceive as a prison for my creativity and earning potential. At that moment, I began working on my plan for escape.

About two years later, I founded Knowsys, a management consulting firm that initially employed only me, as I began to build my business. I worked in earnest to get the company off the ground and was somewhat successful as I was able to create management consulting contracts for myself over the first six months of company start-up.

Even though my earnings were higher than the salary that I had previously made as an employee, my husband was not really onside with my plans. After considerable pressure from him that built upon my fears and insecurities, I decided to go back to work for a large company that offered me a plum job managing a large consulting practice.

Little did I know that my foray back into corporate life would be the best move I ever made to ensure the long-term success of my own business.

Almost immediately after starting my new job, I noticed a recurring pattern. My new boss, the Canadian CEO, would over-ride the decisions of the people who worked for him, yet still hold them responsible for the outcome. This was a phenomenon I had never experienced in all of the companies I had ever worked for.

It quickly became apparent that my new job required that I practically live at work and received midnight emergency calls from my staff and boss, because there was always some crisis to deal with. Basically, these crises were the result of poor management. Proposals to customers were low-balled on cost, not allowing enough time or the right resources to complete the work. When I attempted to reverse this approach, price the work appropriately, and assign senior, experienced resources, I was again over-ruled by my boss and the sales manager who felt that I was difficult to get along with because I never agreed with his pricing strategies.

The result of all this, was that the company I had gone to work for was developing a bad reputation with clients. My good reputation was becoming tainted, simply by association.

When I became very ill with bronchitis and took a week off to recover, my boss' response to me when I came back was that I was not devoted enough to my job and not a team player, because I always disagreed with the Sales team's proposal/pricing approach. He told me that he considered me a marginal performer even though under my management, our staff and profit had tripled in less than six months.

I left his office, went back to mine, closed the door, and began planning my next steps. I would resign immediately and then re-start Knowsys with no holds barred.

Those two events were the catalysts that created the seeds of a business that would blossom and grow over the subsequent ten years, resulting in financial and personal freedom for me and my family, not to mention joy and immense achievement.

I recounted this story because I believe there are a lot of people out there who have faced similar circumstances. Maybe you are facing them right at this moment.

What are some of the Signs?

For many of you who have fantasized or thought seriously about becoming an entrepreneur, there are several specific signs or personal characteristics that would strongly indicate your need and suitability to start your own business.

Limited Career Advancement or Job Loss

You feel like there is nothing new to learn in your current job or that there are limited advancement opportunities in your current company. Perhaps you have been in the same field for many years and feel like you would like to start a completely different career.

Whether they are in your 20's or in your 50's, many entrepreneurs are people who have spent a lot of time in a particular career or field, and have been able to parlay that knowledge into a business of their own. Of course, a growing number of these people are baby-boomers who want a new career instead of traditional "retirement".

Corporate down-sizing and re-structuring constantly "surprises" people with a job loss that is not expected. But out of great adversity and disappointment can the seeds of a new business be sown.

The point here is that some of the most successful entrepreneurs have been those who recognized their career limitations and job losses as opportunities in disguise. These people were able to successfully transfer those skills and knowledge into self-employment or a new business.

Career Success Combined With Poor Physical and Mental Energy

Some people face the opposite problems. They may have tremendous career potential, are on the fast-track, and have achieved considerable financial rewards, but feel depressed, apathetic, lack energy, and are often quite ill.

Sometimes this situation arises when very bright people choose careers they can make a lot of money at, but the job does not really reflect who they are or how they want to live. For example, many successful women who are wives and mothers are phenomenally successful, but their success is at odds with their desire to have more flexibility, the ability to spend more time with their children and/or spouses, or to have more personal time for themselves to pursue their passions in a variety of interests.

Oftentimes, people in this situation will feel trapped or imprisoned, and these strong emotions will manifest themselves in poor physical or mental health. When you think about it, poor health is one of the most effective passive-resistance tools a person can use to avoid doing things they hate but are obligated to do.

I know this first-hand because this became a recurring pattern in my health until I started to get my personal and business life in synch with my values and needs.

Miraculous health improvements take place in people when they decide to pursue their dreams and passions. All of a sudden, working sixty hours a week on a dream invokes superhuman strength. This can be contrasted against working in a job that is toxic or at odds with who you really are, which feels like you are constantly wading through thick mud.

You are a Baby-Boomer Who Sees Your Second Act as an Opportunity for a New Challenge Instead of Retirement

A significant number of potential entrepreneurs are coming from the Baby-Boomers. For many of these affluent people, retirement is right around the corner, but retirement doesn't mean the same thing that we have come to associate with this term.

Retirement for baby-boomers is a second-act. Just think of it. We are all living longer. For a woman in her fifties who has worked all of her adult life in a profession and/or the business world, she potentially has another thirty to fifty years left on this earth. Fun and relaxation are important elements of this next phase, but how much golfing or gardening can a person do and still feel jazzed about life?

Many women see this retirement phase as an opportunity to dive into a completely new profession or their own business (sometimes both).

With excellent financial resources, great intellect, and the capacity to learn, and great health, women are becoming poised to achieve great things as CEO's of their own enterprises.

You are Obsessed with Finding Investment or Money-making Opportunities

You may not necessarily be feeling bad or unfulfilled. Some would-be entrepreneurs are happy in what they are currently doing, but their need to become an entrepreneur is manifested as a desire for alternate channels of income.

For example, these individuals are constantly on the look-out for the next great investment or business opportunity and often will feel envious or like they are missing out on something when they are exposed to someone who has achieved success starting a business and/or achieving their dream.

People in this situation will almost always feel very emotional when watching movies or talk-shows show-casing people who have overcome great adversity to achieve their dreams or passion in life.

There are two movies that stick-out in my mind, during the time I was making my final mental transition from employee to entrepreneur, "Jerry McGuire" (Tom Cruise) and "The Associate" (Whoopy Goldberg). Both these movies were about individuals who had lost their jobs unexpectedly, Jerry McGuire was fired and Whoopy Goldberg's character resigns after being passed over for promotion. Both characters endure highs and lows trying to find a way to get their businesses off the ground and pay the bills. But it is when both characters become true to themselves and operate with a sense of personal commitment, passion, and accountability that their businesses explode with opportunity. These two movies served as inspiration and guides with respect to staying true to my authentic talents. Observing and learning how two very different people in two very different industries handled job loss and being passed over for promotion, reinforced my feelings and experiences as being universal catalysts to getting off my ass and on with my dream.

Basically, both these movies reflected all of my desires, goals, fears, and anxieties about starting my business and revealed a realistic picture of what I could expect. I watched both movies over and over again as a source of inspiration. Each time I watched them, I cried and laughed at the inevitable highs and lows. Within a few months of watching those films, I was on my way to great success in resurrecting Knowsys.

You are a Driven Achiever and Self-Improvement Fanatic

Another clue that you are fated to become the CEO of your own destiny is that you are the personality type that is driven to succeed in everything you do. For example, you don't just jog for exercise, you train for marathons. When you take up a job, hobby, or interest, you do it to perfection and with great passion, commitment, and zeal.

Even when you read for relaxation, it is usually about ways and means to improve your life whether it be business, relationships, health, or spirituality. Biographies of inspirational people have probably always fascinated you.

All of these characteristics can constitute clues with respect to whether you have a natural inclination to become an entrepreneur. If you study great entrepreneurs, most if not all of these people demonstrate these personality traits or interests.

If you are reading this, you are probably contemplating starting your own business but are not sure if this is the path you are meant to take. Some of you have already started your business or have even been at it for many years but are constantly looking for ways to improve your performance or even to start another business venture.

You Come from a Long Line of Entrepreneurs

Don't discount your family history. Chances are if you come from a family of entrepreneurs, you already have many of the characteristics and habits that would potentially set you up for success in your own business.

It was only after I had established Knowsys and it was a going concern for several years that I had an epiphany. I actually had the entrepreneurial DNA from both sides of my family.

The financial success I had achieved allowed me the opportunity to travel extensively. One summer, I took my Mother to Greece to visit her family and to re-connect with my heritage. As I spoke at length with my maternal great aunts, I heard endless stories of their successes running a fashion design/atelier business in Cairo, Egypt, initially and then in Athens. It became apparent that my grandmother and her sisters had done very well with that business, and in point of fact, had single-handedly supported their families when their husbands had lost jobs or became too ill to work.

I actually came from a long line of female entrepreneurs. On top of that, most of my maternal cousins owned their own businesses and were very successful. Becoming aware of these patterns on my Mother's side of the family, I began to review my Dad's family.

Basically, all of my Dad's male relatives—father, and uncles owned their own businesses. My Dad would often tell the story of how his father advised him over and over, to study a profession that would allow him to become self-employed.

My Dad did not end up following his father's advice, but pursued a career as an economist working for large multi-nationals and then the Canadian Federal Government. My Father never felt fulfilled or jazzed by his career, especially in his later years working for the Federal Government. Un-knowingly, I had stored this valuable information away, until I too began to repeat the same patterns of my father—feeling un-fulfilled and energetically bankrupt by the prestigious and high-paying positions I had.

I quickly realized that life was too short to become bored and drained by a job that did not address my vision of how I wanted to live life and how much money I could earn.

Look around you. Do you come from a family that created its livelihood from entrepreneurship? If you do, you probably already have many of the personality characteristics and behaviors that are second nature to the most successful business people. The question is are you going to leverage these family jewels or ignore them.

These anecdotes and entrepreneurial characteristics are all sign posts that can potentially confirm your inclination, fantasies, or very real plans to start your own business. By understanding yourself, you are mastering one of the basic building blocks of your future success. It is up to you to recognize your strengths, fears, interests, and what inspires you. Inspiration will become the seed that will germinate your company into success that you envision.

You Have the Entrepreneurial Personality Profile

After reviewing the biographies of numerous successful entrepreneurs and observing those in my circle of influence, I have come up with a list of personality characteristics for successful entrepreneurs:

1. Optimistic Attitude—entrepreneurs by their very nature are optimists. They believe in the power of possibility. They believe in themselves. They have a strong innate faith that no matter what life throws at them; they will come out on top.
2. It is very difficult to start a profitable business from nothing but an

idea and not be optimistic that you have the qualities to stay the course and turn obstacles into opportunity.

3. Excellent knowledge of human behavior and how to manage it to their desired outcome. Entrepreneurs are keen students of human behavior. They may have spent a good part of their lives trying to figure out what makes people tick and how to leverage this knowledge into something beneficial. Women particularly are socialized to learn how to read people and anticipate behavior in order to get their desired outcome in a way that makes the person think that it was his/her idea.

   Additionally, by understanding human behavior, entrepreneurs understand that nothing is black and white, and as such, know how to bend the "rules" to achieve their desired outcomes. They understand that "marketing" their ideas in a way that addresses their audience's needs is more than just reiterating facts. It is knowing how to spin information, knowledge, and capabilities in such a way as to get customers or employees' attention and commitment.

4. Visionaries who know how to execute. Entrepreneurs know how to dream big and make those dreams a reality. Successful entrepreneurs have a knack of not only coming up with the next great idea, but more importantly how to get the right resources and people in place to actualize their vision.

5. Demanding perfectionists. Successful entrepreneurs are rarely described as easygoing and relaxed. They are more often than not type "A" personalities who never stop moving, never stop achieving, and never stop demanding the best of themselves and those who work with them. Beware the laissez-faire personality around the successful entrepreneur. She will eat those types of individuals for breakfast.

6. Exceptional negotiators. The most successful entrepreneurs are those who believe that everything is negotiable and proceed to do just that. These people have the knack of making the recipient on the other side of the table feel like they are getting what they need out of the negotiation, while at the same time winning major concessions and achieving their objectives at the same time.

7. Natural risk-takers with high self-esteem. The words entrepreneur and risk-taker are almost synonymous. Entrepreneurs have to be

comfortable with putting themselves, their money, and even other people on the line when they are an entrepreneur. There are no guarantees in life, except death of course.

8. Great entrepreneurs are comfortable with taking risks and rely heavily on their belief in themselves to give them the security blanket needed to take chances like investing their own money into a venture, working insane hours to get the business off the ground, and trusting their employees or business partners to do what is necessary to achieve financial and business objectives.

9. Having said all of this, entrepreneurs take calculated risks. All successful businesses were built on the basis of well-understood risks and benefits. Taking risks just for the sake of excitement or greed are not part of the make-up of top notch entrepreneurs.

10. Entrepreneurs are not afraid of a good fight. All successful entrepreneurs know and love the idea that they will compete against small or sometimes giant corporations to grow their business. They know and understand the need for competition. They look upon this part of the business landscape as their ability to survive and grow amidst obstacles, pressure, and uncertainty and still come out in a profitable position.

Take a completely honest look at yourself-your characteristics-strengths and weaknesses. There are many signs around you giving you direction as to your true calling, next act, or greatest dreams. Pay attention to these signs and take the time to really know yourself. When you feel you have a good sense of your aptitude to be an entrepreneur, take it to the next step. Look for your true inspiration!

CHAPTER 2
Finding Your True Inspiration

Some of the greatest ideas and business ventures started with imagination, dreams, and inspiration. How do you determine what your business will look like, what products or services you will sell? How do you determine what business will both interest you and make money?

The answers to these potentially mind-boggling questions are know yourself very, very well and understand what truly inspires you.

In other words, the better you know yourself, your weaknesses and strengths, anxieties and dreams, what bores and what inspires you, the better-equipped you will be to start a successful business.

Inspiration is defined as arousal of the mind to special, unusual activity or creativity. It is also the sudden intuition as part of solving a problem.

During the ten years that I contemplated what kind of business I would start, I began focusing more and more on what truly inspired me. I also examined what activities or experiences excited me and propelled me to my highest performance. I constantly questioned myself about what unique qualities I possessed and how I could turn them into money.

I began to devour books on the subject of self-development/improvement, sales skills, attracting prosperity into your life, living an inspired life. During this time, I began to formulate my vision of how I wanted to live life, what I wanted to achieve for myself and my family.

Steven Covey, author of *The Seven Habits of Successful People*, recommends "starting with the end in mind." What is your vision for your best future? What are your major life goals? If you don't know the answer to these questions, it may be very difficult to determine the direction and focus of your business.

How do you go about finding the answers to these life altering questions?

There are several practical methods and tools you can use to determine what inspires you and how to turn that inspiration into a viable business. Some of these tools include:

- Dream Board
- "100" Life Goals
- Research
- Meditation and Prayer
- Listening to Your Intuition
- Networking

Dream Board

An excellent tool to help you really understand what is important to you and what inspires you is to create a dream board or book. A dream board is a collection of images, photographs, articles that documents what you want out of life.

A dream board is very easy to put together. You simply cut out pictures of things you want, interest, or fascinate you. For example, you may cut out photos of your dream house, vacation, hobbies, places that fascinate you, sports that intrigue you, perhaps even photos of your ideal mate or family. The dream board is only limited by your imagination.

You can create a large board and put it up on a wall where you work or exercise. In addition, or alternatively, you can put together a book you continually add to and review on a regular basis.

A scrapbook/journal allows you to organize your thoughts, ideas, images that inspire you or that you aspire to. A scrapbook can be an excellent tool to document the process by which you develop ideas that can be subsequently marketed.

The value of this exercise is that it allows you to see what you really want out of life. It also may give you clues with respect to patterns of your interests and dreams. If for example, your dream board is focused upon nature and artistic interests, perhaps starting a business that allows you to relocate to the country or gives you the opportunity for flexibility in terms of where you work may be an important clue to consider.

We have all heard the stories of famous people who wrote themselves cheques or letters as of a particular date in the future and then miraculously achieved those goals (or income very close to that listed on their cheque) by that date.

I remember an anecdote of a successful businessman/entrepreneur who had just moved into a gorgeous estate. He was unpacking boxes to set-up his office when his young son walked in. His son helped him unpack one of the boxes and in it found a board with many photographs and quotes glued to it. He asked his father what it was. His father explained that it was a "dream board" and explained how he used the board as a tool in achieving his objectives.

As the father and son were talking about this subject, the father unpacked another board, and as he looked at it, he began to weep. The board depicted pictures of a gorgeous home and estate that the businessman had pieced together four years before. The pictures were those of the home and estate he was currently moving into. He had actualized his dream down to the exact detail of acquiring the same home as was in those photographs.

The point here is that visioning, that is creating a specific picture in your mind of what you want to achieve whether it is sports performance, relationships, or financial success is a necessary element for every entrepreneur. Remember back to the description of successful entrepreneurs—they are visionaries who actualize their dreams. This is one tool you can use to create the mental focus and vision necessary to achieve your dreams.

"100" Life Goals

Another tool every person should make use of whether or not you are a CEO is the technique of writing down your one-hundred major life goals. As an entrepreneur and CEO this is a practice that should be done on a regular basis, at least once every three months.

Basically, what you do is write down each goal that you have, describing what it is and when you plan to achieve it. By reviewing these goals regularly, you can actually see your progress—what you have achieved against what you have planned.

When you take a look at your goals, patterns will emerge. Your values, priorities, interests, and passions will provide you with important clues as to where your strengths and aptitudes lie.

In addition, when you understand what you want to achieve in your life and then you determine what kind of business you want to start, the two pieces must be compatible. If they are not in synch, you will have to make adjustments in your life.

Research

Once you have identified a business opportunity, you will need to do some thorough research in order to validate the feasibility of taking the plunge of investing your time, money, heart, and soul in that business.

Some characteristics of business opportunities that you should evaluate closely are:

1. Does the product or service fill a need that is not currently being addressed?
2. Does the product or service create value for its customers, so that they will pay even a premium price for it?
3. Is the projected profit enough that it makes the potential risk worth taking?
4. Is there a good fit between the opportunity and your capabilities or areas of knowledge and experience?
5. Can you devote your life and actually get passionate about the business opportunity?

In order to determine which business opportunity you should go after, doing a WOTS analysis—weaknesses, opportunities, threats, and strengths can be very useful.

Weaknesses are classified as drawbacks or areas of vulnerability in your product or service offering. Your analysis should be geared at understanding the weaknesses of your business idea and how you will mitigate these weaknesses.

Opportunities are areas of potential revenue or customers that could be developed to use the potential product or service.

Threats are factors outside of the company that could threaten or jeopardize the viability of your company/business idea. They include competition, the economy, regulations, demographics, or the political landscape that your business may be impacted by.

Strengths are differentiators or core competencies of your company, product and/or service. Understanding your strengths allows you to develop or build upon your business idea by maximizing those capabilities.

Any research you do must be targeted upon finding the facts and evidence to support or negate the weaknesses, opportunities, threats, and strengths of your business.

Areas to research in order to better understand threats are:
1. the economy
2. the political landscape
3. regulatory changes
4. social change
5. competition

There are many different sources you can use for your research. Some of these include:
- The internet
- Industry Associations
- Magazines, books, and other periodicals
- CEO's or executives in the business you wish to start
- University Professors who are experts in the industry you are looking to enter
- Your commercial banker

Listening to Your Intuition

I believe that as women, we have developed highly-honed intuition that we habitually ignore.

Learning to trust your intuition is very difficult, but extremely necessary if you are going to run your own business. You must learn to read between the lines of human behavior and verbiage, to understand what is really going on behind the scenes.

For example, have you ever had an overwhelming feeling that you needed to take action, or speak to someone at a particular moment, or hold back on making a decision, and then found that this intuition served you particularly well—opening up an opportunity or safeguarding you from potential problems?

We have all had these moments. However, most women distrust their intuition—especially business women. They try to use logic, almost to the exclusion of their intuition. If this is a behavior pattern of yours, you will need to work hard to trust your inner voice and take the leap of faith.

I was one of those women who tried to ignore my inner voice and focused instead on logic. Unfortunately, every time I ignored my intuition, I betrayed my best interests and those of my company. After proverbially "burning my fingers" several times, I made a conscious decision to go with my intuition and act decisively on these hunches.

Listening to my intuition allowed me to start my business at the perfect time from a business/economic cycle—even though my logic told me that I didn't have the finances or secured customers before I resigned from my lucrative six-figure salary.

Listening to my inner voice allowed me to hire some of the best and brightest people I have ever had the privilege of working with. Ignoring my inner voice actually created legal repercussions with employees and contractors who proved to be unethical and an actual threat to the viability of my business.

Listening to my instincts allowed me to meet with new and existing customers at the right time, so that we would immediately sign new business contracts. Similarly, great investments were made when I acted on my instincts. The opposite was true when I handed over my decision-making power to investment advisors who helped me to lose hundreds of thousands of dollars.

Listening and following my intuition has allowed me to foresee potential health problems for my family and to mitigate the risks or dangers of these problems by consulting with doctors or other health professionals in advance of a health problem becoming so acute that it could not be solved.

So the point of this section is to remind you to listen to your inner voice, emotions, and physical sensations when you are in different situations. Pay attention. Experiment with taking action on your intuition or fighting it and using your logic. See what happens in each scenario and learn from these experiences and apply your knowledge to new challenges.

Use your intuition to understand or focus your attention on potential business opportunities that not only make sense logically but also feel right. By being very aware of your hunches and acting upon them, you will find that opportunities and coincidences will abound where you seem to meet the right person at the right time to help you actualize your dreams.

"All the women leaders I have met led with a greater sense of intuition than men. I am almost completely intuitive. The only time I've made a bad business decision is when I didn't follow my instinct. My favorite phrase is: 'Let me pray on it.' Sometimes I literally do pray, but sometimes I just wait to see if I wake up and feel the same way in the morning. For me, doubt normally means don't. Doubt means do nothing until you know what to do." Oprah Winfrey, *Newsweek*, October 24, 2005.

Meditation and Prayer

Most people would look at the category of meditation and prayer and wonder why it even has a place in a guide to entrepreneurship. From my perspective, meditation and prayer was one of the most important tools I used in determining what business I would develop and how I would go about making it a success. As you can see from Oprah Winfrey's quote, she is another successful entrepreneur who leans heavily on spiritual tools to guide her progress and success.

For those of you who are religious, you can look at both elements. For those of you who are not religious or even spiritual, you can still benefit from using meditation.

Prayer is a tool I use to help me focus my spiritual and mental energy amidst the doubts and trials that life brings my way each day. Prayer opens my mind and soul, and allows me to become receptive to inspiration. Prayer centers me and allows me to concentrate on whatever I need to do to get my job done or my business to the next level. It also helps to guide my interactions with clients and employees who are not always easy to be in sync with.

Prayer is also a tool that helps me realize that if I am focusing on what is just good for me, I have moved away from the right path with respect to why I started and grew my company. I believe that the growth of my company is part of a spiritual journey that allows me to enrich not only myself and my family but all those who this business touches. Prayer reminds me of this mission and changes my mental attitude, especially when I must accomplish something important within the context of a meeting or a presentation to a client.

Meditation is a tool that accomplishes so many benefits. Meditation improves my physical and mental health. It improves my energy levels and ability to focus my mind. It allows me to listen to my inner voice and also information that the universe is sending me, but which I may not hear, amidst all the noise that surrounds my life.

There are numerous books and techniques to help you figure out how to meditate. I have included several references in the reading list at the back of this book.

There are universal principles that apply to meditation. You need to go to a physical place that is quiet. You take a few minutes each day to quiet your mind or to use images, symbols, or visioning to create a sense of peace or empowerment.

After you have become extremely quiet, you can ask yourself questions about whether or not you should take a particular decision or will that decision pan out the way you are hoping. You will start to become aware of answers coming back to your questions that either resonate with "rightness" or stimulate knots in your stomach and create uncertainty and doubt. If your body is reacting unfavorably to the questions you are asking of yourself, you might need to meditate further before taking any action. I believe that your body and soul already know a lot of the answers to the questions that nag your confidence or the hard decisions that you need to make but are uncertain about.

Networking
Networking is another powerful tool that you can use in your bag of tricks to bring you the inspiration, ideas, or people to help you make your business a reality or allowing you to take your business to the next level of development.

There are many ways you can use networking to jumpstart your inspirational engine.

You can approach networking from several angles:
- Join associations that are focused upon supporting and developing female entrepreneurs;
- Get involved with associations that are related to the profession or business that you are involved in;
- Attend business events where your customers are likely to be

and where you can develop contacts and acquaintances without the pressure of a sales situation;

- Become a member of a health and/or golf club where you can develop acquaintances and friendships with other entrepreneurs or potential clients. For example, you might develop an acquaintance that works in one of the companies you want to target as a potential client. There are all kinds of informal information that an acquaintance such as this might pass on casually or specifically that will allow you to learn something valuable about your profession or target customer base.
- Leverage an already existing membership you have within your church, synagogue, or mosque. You would be surprised by how much people within religious denominations go out of their way to help others—even if it is business-related.

There are many ways to find inspiration and turn your dreams into an actionable business plan. Experiment with all of these approaches. Note down your ideas in a journal.When a particular idea or theme seems to repeat itself or resonate with you,your inspiration is letting you know what path you need to follow.

CHAPTER 3
Taking Personal Inventory

Ok, so you are finally inspired, you have determined what your business will be and what products or services you will be selling. In other words, you have a solid concept, but no business plan yet. Before you dive into your business plan, there is one very important task you need to work through carefully. This task is doing a personal inventory.

What is a personal inventory you are probably asking? Doing a personal inventory for yourself can be compared to preparing and training for a marathon.

You don't just go out and run a marathon. You have to understand what level of physical fitness you are currently at. You need to understand what kind of training and preparation is required. You may need to join a running group in order to prepare for the marathon. You will need to consult with a nutritionist and put yourself on a regimented eating plan that will fuel your intense exercise, maintain your muscle, and yet keep you lean and light. You will also need to do significant mental preparation to help you train your mind and body to work in concert with one another instead of at odds with each other. And of course, you will have to train and practice with consistency and discipline, even when you don't feel like it.

So let's go back to the concept of doing your personal inventory. It is very much the same thing. You need to assess your strengths and weaknesses, assets and liabilities, vision and value, priorities, and tolerance for risk. In the process of assessing your capabilities, you will also have to think about the interventions or "training" that you will need to get you into physical, mental, and financial shape to allow you to carry your business plan forward into reality.

Your personal inventory should consist of these categories of assessment:

- Character/Personality Strengths and Weaknesses (including mental/psychological characteristics);
- Education or Work Experience Related to Business;
- Financial Health-assets, cash, retirement savings, income from other sources, adjustments required;
- Family Situation Assessment—responsibilities—children, husband, aged parents, disabilities/illnesses of your own; and
- Availability of Mentors or Coaches for support and guidance—informal and formal.

Character/Personality Strengths and Weaknesses

When you assess your character/personality strengths and weaknesses you are basically taking an honest look at yourself and determining if you have what it really takes to pursue your business idea through to its successful culmination.

Use some of the meditation, prayer, and intuition skills you have been working on and apply them by sitting down in a very quiet place and asking yourself the questions—who am I? What are the characteristics of my personality and character? What are my strengths and weaknesses?

Answer these questions by writing your answers in point-form and under the relevant categories. For example, list all your strengths under the category of strengths. Review your points. What patterns or messages do you get about your abilities? What patterns begin to emerge with respect to your "weaknesses"?

The next step is take these notes and review them with someone you trust completely, someone who is not afraid to tell you the truth—the good, bad, and the ugly.

It may be obvious to you or the person(s) you review your assessment with, that you are the next Martha Stewart or Bill Gates. On the other hand, if you have personality characteristics that are obviously contrary to those of a business person, for example you lack discipline or never follow through on your commitments or objectives, perhaps you might need to re-think your objectives or work very hard to surround yourself with people who can mitigate your deficiencies.

A very good example of this type of challenge, and one I might add that is common to many entrepreneurs, is that many CEO's are fabulous visionaries but are not terribly good at execution. If this is your case, you will definitely need someone who is your second in command, who you can delegate all of your great ideas to and know that they will make them happen.

By the same token, many entrepreneurs are control-freaks. They think that if something is to be done right, they must do it themselves and therefore quickly get burned out doing too much, and in the end accomplishing nothing. If you see similar characteristics in your character or past behavior, you will need to work very hard from the get-go at delegating work to people whom you can trust to follow-through.

So, the basic premise of this exercise is not for you to learn that you are not cracked-up for entrepreneurship, but for you to be intimately aware of what your deficiencies and assets are, and surround yourself with the people, knowledge, and resources to maximize your strengths and minimize or manage your weaknesses.

Education or Work Experience

Taking stock of your education and work experience is another logical step in taking a full personal inventory.

Take a good hard look at your education and training. Is it relevant to the business you plan to invest in. If it is great; if it isn't, do you need to take some additional training or education before you embark upon this business?

Or does your career and work experience more than compensate for your lack of education? Many people fall into this category. In fact, some of the most successful entrepreneurs we know and celebrate did not have formal education or training in the business they eventually pioneered.

However, you may or may not have the alternatives that these people had. Should his business not have taken-off, I'm sure that Bill Gates could have easily gone back to Harvard with his parents' full blessing and financial support. You may not have those options open to you at this stage in the game.

Therefore, take a good hard look at your skills and experience, and again formulate a balance sheet based upon your education, training, and work experience. Again, the point of this exercise is to focus upon what you are exceptionally good at and make sure that your role in the business takes advantage of your exceptional knowledge and strengths.

At the same time, if you are deficient in knowledge or experience in critical areas, you will either need to get that experience, which might mean going back to school for a period of time, or it might mean recruiting people with these areas of knowledge to fill in your "gaps." Some entrepreneurs will have the luxury of hiring their "A" team with all of the complementary knowledge, experience, and qualities to maximize the company's efficacy. Others will not have this option and will need to either learn these skills quickly or contract that knowledge on an as-and when-required basis.

In terms of continuing education and training, you can go the traditional route of attending classes in a particular location, or you can do an on-line degree, course, or certification where you can learn at home and in the evenings, allowing you to continue working during the daytime.

Financial Health

What is your current financial picture? Do you know? Do you intimately understand what assets, cash, and liabilities you possess? Are you willing to take calculated risks with your money or your family's money?

These are probably some of the most difficult questions to ponder because they essentially make you "put your money where your mouth is" so to speak. It is one thing to come up with a great business idea. It is quite another to actually decide to use your hard-earned savings or retirement savings or your husband's savings to ignite your business.

I remember a very relevant conversation I had with one of my mentors, a man by the name of Harvey Gellman, who recently passed away. He was a multi-millionaire in my industry, had started his business with his own two hands and cash, and then sold it to a large, public Canadian company that became a multi-billion dollar, global enterprise.

When I asked him how he started his company, he recounted the experience for me.

"Mary-Ann," he said, "You have to be prepared to make sacrifices and get rid of things you have worked hard to attain."

"Can you explain what you mean Harvey, I don't understand?" I asked him with great consternation.

"You have to be willing to get rid of all of your debts-like a mortgage for example. When I started Gellman and Hayward, my wife and I rented an apartment and lived very, very frugally.

Are you willing to get rid of your mortgage and rent an apartment or home, Mary-Ann?"

"I am not sure, Harvey. That is a really big question. I will need to discuss that with my husband and determine if he is willing to do so."

At that time, my husband and I were newly married, had just bought a beautiful home in Ottawa that we were currently renting to tenants because we were living and working in Toronto. My husband and I had several decisions to make. Did we want to start the business in Toronto or Ottawa? Should we sell our house?

In the end we sold our house in Ottawa and decided to rent a home in Toronto, but not before we had moved back and forth between the two cities trying to figure out which location would give us a better chance at success.

You will need to understand your financial situation intimately. You will need to discuss how you will get rid of all or as much of your personal debt as possible, before you start your company.

You will need to understand how much it currently costs you to live the lifestyle you are accustomed to. There may be some pretty serious adjustments ahead to that lifestyle, once your business is being birthed. You will need to get agreement from your spouse with respect to cutting back on unnecessary expenses—vacations, eating out, and expensive clothing or hobbies.

These will be difficult discussions with your husband or partner, because they will put your values, beliefs, and priorities about money to the test. Ultimately, you will see if you and your spouse are on the same page with respect to the financial sacrifices, investments, and risks that will need to be taken to make your business a reality.

Specific things you will need to do to get your financial house in order are:

1. Prepare a budget for living and stick to it. Eliminate all unnecessary and discretionary expenses and debt-credit cards are a big one.

2. Learn to pay off all of your debts each month with cash—not debt. This will be an important behavior to master because it will also help you manage your business' cash position successfully.

3. Use sources of income that you are completely comfortable cashing in. In other words, if you cashed in your retirements savings today and knew that there was a definite possibility that you could lose part or all of it, could you actually sleep at night and focus on building your business?

4. Write down your financial plan and get your spouse to sign his agreement on it so that, down the line, if there are any problems, which we know there always are, you will have the proof to quiet-down concerns or blame.

Family Situation Assessment

Starting and building a business can be compared to doing battle each day, conquering your fears, competitors, winning over new customers, and mobilizing your employees to act in concert with your business objectives.

I cannot emphasize enough, how important your family life will be in determining how well you can focus upon building your business. If your family situation is unstable or un-supportive of the responsibilities and time you will need to devote to your new venture, your business and family's viability could be in serious danger.

As part two of the finance discussion with your spouse, also discuss his expectations with respect to how much time you will be available to spend with him and the children, as you are getting the business off the ground, and once it is running full steam ahead. You might be very surprised at the expectations of your spouse in this area. Some spouses rally behind dreams and the sacrifices required to make them happen. Others will fold or turn tail at the slightest challenge or added responsibilities at home.

If you are a stay-at-home mother and are starting your own business, be sure to plan for solid daycare and housekeeping, even cooking while you are focused upon your new business. For those women who have always worked and have employed nannies or daycare, don't get fooled into thinking that you can do it all just because you are working out of the house. That will not be the case, I assure you.

For those women whose children are in university or already working and living outside the home, be aware of your husband's expectations with how much time you will be or not be at home. You may be very surprised at the reactions and expectations of your spouses when you have pointed, crystal-clear discussions about each person's roles and responsibilities.

My point is this is. Discuss everything. Write down your plan, roles and responsibilities, and parachute clauses. Be flexible and realistic and make sure your spouse understands the upside and downside of your time commitments before you start pouring your heart and soul into the new business venture.

The assumption here is not that you need to take your husband's permission to move forward on your dreams, but you do need his commitment and buy-in to being part of your support team. If that support is missing, you will not be able to focus on building your business successfully.

Availability of Mentors or Coaches

If you examine the biographies of very successful entrepreneurs, you will be struck with the critical importance of mentors or coaches. These people have played the roles of teachers, advisors, devil's advocates, and cheerleaders in helping shape the entrepreneur's confidence, instincts, and skills at important checkpoints in their company's evolution.

What is a mentor or a coach? A mentor or coach is someone who formally or informally acts as a guide for your move through each stage of the development of your company and your abilities as a CEO.

The difference for me, between a mentor and a coach, is that a mentor is someone who provides you with advice as part of a personal relationship and mutual respect. Mentors don't charge you for their time in advising you, they do it because they feel a personal loyalty and care for your success as a business person.

A professional coach is someone you pay for specific, well-defined services that you can use to develop your leadership qualities and/or business success.

How do you go about finding a mentor or coach? Depending upon the business you go into, that can be a very difficult or a reasonably easy task. The more specialized or complex your business is, the more important, if not critical, the role of your mentor.

I have found mentors in the form of older and wiser colleagues or even ex-bosses who had an honest rapport with me, and whose opinion and knowledge was well-respected by the industry as a whole.

I have also tapped into a variety of professionals that serve my business: accountants, lawyers, commercial and retail bankers, recruiters, real estate brokers, public relations, and even information technology people (those who helped design our website).

There are actually specialized mentor associations or sub-committees as part of professional associations that you might already belong to that are focused upon seeding entrepreneurial talent. You can research these options through the internet or by asking your banker or lawyer.

A professional coach is a little different than a mentor. A professional coach is someone whom you pay to give you advice and knowledge that will enrich your ability as leader or manager, or who will give you an un-biased third-party opinion of a decision or strategy you would like to take but are not sure about.

Either way, with either type of advisor, you will need their help at all junctions in your journey to becoming a successful CEO and running a profitable company. The key is to always be on the lookout for these people and to always maintain an open mind with respect to new ideas, strategies, even advice that you might not like to hear.

The quality of your mentors and coaches will have a direct impact on your success as an entrepreneur. Your ability to recognize, listen, and actualize their advice when it is warranted could make the difference between becoming a self-made millionaire or simply scraping by.

We have examined whether you have the personality characteristics of an entrepreneur, discovered sources of inspiration to architect your dream business, and have assessed your personal preparedness to execute. Now we are going to dive into the cold waters of reality and articulate a business plan to bring your dreams to fruition.

CHAPTER 4
Preparing Your Business Plan

Your business plan is the culmination of tremendous analysis and research, introspection, and imagination. The business plan will integrate and document the rationale and evidence supporting your business. Whether you are starting a bakery or a high-tech company, you will need to cover the same components. The only difference between those two business plans will be the level of detail and complexity in the financial sections.

The business plan should be simple and relevant to the business you plan to start. Understanding who your audience is will determine the level of detail and the supporting evidence you will require. If you are boot-strapping your business, the audience for your business plan is you.

If you are looking for funding from the bank, your business plan will need to focus on how you will pay back or service the debt that you are seeking from the bank. Therefore, this plan will be focused upon a conservative view of your potential revenue and what low-risk assets (such as cash or blue-chip accounts receivable) you will be able to use as collateral to finance your line of credit or loan.

If you are looking to receive investments from private investors or venture capitalists, your business plan will need to be quite formal, detailed, and bullet-proof. It will focus upon detailed forecasts of revenue and expense and the rationale to prove the likelihood of a very high rate of return for your potential investors. Every business plan contains the same components, only the level of detail and complexity will vary:

- Business Mission—your company's purpose
- Business Values—the guiding principles
- Objectives and Goals—long/short term actions
- Products and Services to be offered
- Value Proposition—what differentiates you?

- Market Analysis—WOTS
- Proposed Organizational Structure—Management Team
- Financial Analysis—Revenue, Cost, and Profitability Analysis

Business Mission

Your business mission is a clear statement about what business you are in, what you intend to achieve, how you will achieve it, what customers you will target, and how you will differentiate your products and/or services from similar companies. For example, here is my company's mission statement:

Knowsys Group provides business strategy, organization, program management, technology, IT and business process improvement consulting services. Knowsys provides services to the financial services, utilities, and government sectors. Key differentiators of our firm are that all of our consulting personnel are senior executives who have "done it before," but who use Knowsys standard best practices to create high-quality and consistent results every time.

You should be able to use your mission statement as your elevator pitch, to concisely describe the business you are in and the value that you bring to your customers.

Business Values

Your company's business values are akin to the values that you or your family espouses. These business values will be the guiding principles upon which your company culture will be built and will evolve from. Your business values will lay the foundation for your customer's expectations and ultimately for the reputation you develop with customers, employees, vendors, and investors.

Some examples of Knowsys Group's business values are:

Substance, Relevance, Results

External Perspective
Substance
Provide the people and expertise that are equivalent or better than that of the industry leaders at the responsible price.

Relevance

Bring the most forward-thinking, industry-specific knowledge, learning, and methodologies to fast-track our ability to deliver a solution to the customer's problem.

Results

Bring experts who have "done it before" and can successfully execute strategy to create measurable results.

Internal Perspective

Substance

Provide the best compensation, mentally challenging, and meaningful engagements to our consultants. Create a working environment that is collegial, collaborative, and flexible.

Relevance

Value people for their contributions and accomplishments, respect their need to balance family and work to their individual needs and timelines.

Create an environment that is entrepreneurial and pragmatic, while minimizing bureaucracy and politics.

Results

Provide the required templates, tools, and methodologies to minimize duplication of effort and to create superior quality deliverables.

Objectives and Goals

Most people get a little confused between objectives and goals. Goals are broader and more general; they are also more long-term in nature. Objectives are measurable steps to achieve your goals.

Goals provide a framework for more detailed levels of planning. Goals are more specific than the mission statement but remain general enough to stimulate creativity and innovation. They indicate the general changes that will have taken place in the agency, program, or subprogram. Goals describe the "to be" state. The goal can also be described as the end result, generally after three or more years.

Goals will also represent immediate or serious problems or high-priority issues that merit special attention. These critical or strategic issues, which are often uncovered during the internal/external assessment, might be described as the "make or break" kinds of issues.

Objectives: specific and measurable targets for accomplishing goals.

In contrast to goals, objectives are specific, quantifiable and time-bound statements of desired accomplishments or results. As such, objectives represent intermediate achievements necessary to realize goals.

In fact, there is an acronym you can use to define your goals, it is called SMART:
S—Specific
M—Measurable
A—Attainable
R—Results-oriented
T—Time-bound

So, let me give you another example of a goal. Drawing from the sales objectives you have set, you might set a sales goal of achieving $1 million in revenue for a specific software product in 12 months (by the end of your fiscal year) in a particular customer account.

Utilize objectives to lay out what you will achieve from a sales, human resources, customer penetration, customer service, and expense management perspective. Your goals will be specific to each category and may be attributed to specific people on your management team, who will be accountable for achieving both the objectives and goals set out.

The psychology of setting objectives and goals is really important, regardless of whether your business is funded by your own cash or capital, or by other's capital. The act of setting objectives, communicating them, getting agreement from your team in achieving them, and monitoring people's success in achieving these objectives and goals will determine how your organization will behave and how effective you will be in achieving the results that you have envisioned. These results will also need to be tied to the compensation system you implement. Compensation must support and encourage the results you seek to achieve. If you don't take this into consideration, you may have a team that will not be motivated to achieve the objectives and goals you have set out.

Products and Services to be offered

Will you be selling a product or a service or both? A spa sells both, for example, a pedicure and facial, and the products to maintain the health of the skin on your face and your feet.

You will need to prepare a detailed description of the products and or services you plan to market and sell. In a simpler business like a bakery, a detailed list of products will correspond to the raw materials or ingredients you will need to account for from a cost-perspective.

In a more complex business model, describing the management consulting services coupled with the technology products that support them, constitutes another type of product/service description. In addition to the services described, you will also need to create a comprehensive set of activities, deliverables/products, and costs to correspond with the activities and products required to complete the final outcome.

So, the message here is describe every product and service you will sell in excruciating detail, because you will need to match costs and projected revenues to these elements. This will allow you to complete your financial forecasts in more detail and with a higher degree of accuracy.

Value Proposition

The value proposition is essentially what will differentiate your product and service from your competitors' offerings. It also addresses what aspects of your product that will draw new customers or attract customers to buy your offering.

The value proposition must either provide additional features or benefits for the same price or less than that of your competitor's offering. In some cases, you will be able to charge a premium for your offering, if there is nothing like it in the market, or if you are targeting a particular niche, or if you are providing so many additional features or benefits than your competitors.

Basically, whether you are selling apple pies or the next wonder drug, you must intuitively and logically be able to describe the benefit you are adding to people's lives, or the gap or need you are filling, or how you are going to reduce your customer's costs.

Your description of the value proposition of your products and services must be backed up by a thorough market analysis. The description of your market analysis is essentially the set of assumptions and proof, backing up the viability of your business.

Market Analysis

The market analysis for your business is something that should not be new to you. As part of your preparation, you have already done market research on your business idea.

This version is basically a more formal set of assumptions and evidence to support your business strategy. It basically consists of what is referred to as a WOTS analysis. WOTS stands for weaknesses, opportunities, threats, and strengths.

Weaknesses are areas of vulnerability of your product or service with respect to your own organization. Examples of weaknesses are lack of track record in selling the product or service, lack of capital, skilled resources, or references within the customer base you would like to target.

Opportunities are really about revenue, market penetration, customer retention, quality management, and how to leverage these assets into additional revenue or profit.

Threats are related to factors outside of your business such as competition, economic cycles, political impacts, regulatory changes, foreign exchange and interest rate changes and how they can potentially impact your business.

Strengths are assets or capabilities within your organization such as your management team, customer success stories, the robustness of your product, your value-add or value proposition, your responsiveness to customer needs, or your low overhead. These are some of the inherent factors that constitute inherent capabilities and advantages of your company.

It is very important to understand how all these pieces fit together, in order to determine the best business strategy that will put the odds in your favor of achieving financial success. This analysis is basically the empirical evidence that supports the basis for your business.

Proposed Organizational Structure—Management Team

As CEO of your company, you need to understand how important your management team is to the success of your business. Whether you are a "Mom and Pop" shop like a convenience store or a global software company, the right people will make or break the success of your business endeavor.

One of the exercises you already went through is your personal inventory. By taking a good, hard look at your weaknesses or those things you don't like to do or are not good at doing, you will be able to zone in on the kinds of people you will need.

For example, a strong financial/accounting person will be critical to your business from many different angles. This person will focus upon getting your receivables in quickly, managing your costs, keeping a keen eye out for your cash position, and managing your corporate taxation requirements. They will also ensure that all government/taxation paper work is filled out and up to date and ensure that all of your tax payments are made properly and promptly, thereby minimizing potential tax problems later on down the road when you least expect it and can ill afford it.

In addition to your internal accounting person, you will need an excellent accounting firm, as they will work closely with your tax lawyers in determining the best corporate legal structures to minimize tax liability and maximize future capital gains. The accounting firm will also be incredibly important throughout the whole annual corporate taxation cycle and will help to ensure that you don't pay any more or any less than you should to the government.

Another key position is the person who will head up sales and/or marketing. This may in fact be you. But if it isn't, make sure you hire someone with a proven track-record in the business you are in. They should already have established contacts and relationships in place, as opposed to developing those on your dime. If they are heading up product management or marketing make sure that they have done the same thing before for a very similar product or service.

If you are looking for investment capital from outsiders, a finance person with proven experience in raising capital, whether it is from the banks or venture capitalists, will be a necessary investment that potentially will ensure the viability of your company.

An excellent lawyer/law firm that is on retainer for your company will also be another key member of your organization. The role of the lawyer is initially to help you set-up your corporation and its holding companies to minimize tax and personal liabilities. You will also probably require several different types of contracts, for example, employee, customer, and sub-contractor contracts to name a few.

The expertise required from a legal perspective might be quite diverse. For example, at the beginning when you set-up your corporation(s) you will require tax lawyers. When you are looking to establish labor and customer contracts you may need labor or corporate lawyers. For any potential or actual litigation, you will require an excellent corporate litigation lawyer.

If you decide to go public or even just to protect your interests with respect to outside investors, you will also need a lawyer that specializes in these areas.

I advise going to one large law firm that can accommodate all your needs in one place, if that is possible. It will greatly simplify your life.

An excellent investment advisor, both from a personal and corporate perspective will be critical as well. This is because it is so easy to make money, spend it, and have nothing to show for it at the end of the day. I strongly advise all new CEO's to get their investment house in order from the get-go. Get accustomed to saving a significant portion of your income from the business and learning how to invest it wisely, so that you can create other income-creation opportunities to diversify your business risk.

A strong human resources person whom you hire either permanently or on retainer will be invaluable for selection, recruitment, training, and management of your resources. Again, depending upon your business model, you may have limited or significant need for this type of resource. If you have a significant need for this type of resource, but money is limited, hire them on contract or retainer.

Information technology is a necessity to support your business for virtually every organization whether you are a one-man band or are a sizeable team. This capability can be hired on contract or retainer on an "as and when" required basis.

You can employ this approach for almost every key position if you like, since initially you may not have the ability to make long-term commitments with respect to employees. Everyone can be hired on contract initially and then, as revenue streams become more solid, you can choose to hire full-time employees for the most critical positions.

Although your banker is not technically part of your management team, make them a virtual component of your team. I cannot emphasize enough how important it is to hire a good banker who is compatible with your mentality and values and who will go out on a limb for you when you will need it. The secret to a good relationship here is to always honor your commitments and create a track record which substantiates your trust worthiness from a credit risk perspective. You may need both a personal banker and a corporate banker, as one may give you additional leeway at certain junctions in your credit maturity lifecycle, whereas another may not have the same latitude.

Finally, don't under-estimate the need for an excellent insurance advisor. You need to consider things like disability, critical illness insurance, and life insurance on a personal and business basis. You may require a life insurance policy that you pay for as an individual to protect the potential income and current expenses that would fall on your family if you died. You may also require additional insurance that is paid out by your company to cover the losses incurred by the company and the salary of the person required to replace you in the event of your death. These are morose things to think about; however, if you don't think about them and do something to address these risks, then your family will pay a heavy price in the event of your death. I think that is the last thing anyone, especially a mother, would ever do to their family. Therefore, be realistic, think ahead, and protect your family's interests, in case the unthinkable were to happen.

Determining a compensation or retainer schedule that minimizes cost and liability to the company, but at the same time motivates your team to achieve the objectives and goals that you have set out together, will be a critical piece of your business strategy.

Financial Analysis—Revenue, Cost, and Profitability Analysis

The rule of thumb here is the more complex your business model, the more detailed your financials and the assumptions underlying them should be.

You need to establish sales revenue forecasts that are realistic and based upon solid assumptions. These assumptions should be within your span of control rather than based on factors that are outside of your reach.

Your sales projections should be done on a monthly basis and if possible, mapped out against specific customer accounts. Any other substantiating evidence, such as previous experience with similar products in like markets will be very pertinent.

Underneath your sales projections, are those wonderful elements we call costs or expenses. Again, you will need to be very detailed with every element required to support your business.

Some examples of cost categories you can utilize are as follows:

- Salaries, benefits, and bonuses
- Rent and lease expense for office space
- Utilities
- Legal and Accounting fees
- Recruitment fees
- Travel
- Entertainment
- Education and Training
- Marketing Promotion
- Supplies
- Computer Hardware
- Computer Software
- Furniture
- Leasehold Improvements

If you are funding your own company, your financials are a tool that you and your accountant will be using to manage your cash position and your day-to-day operations. If on the other hand, you are seeking funding from the bank, they will ask you for additional detail and/or revenue/expense forecasts. If you are looking for venture capital, you may need to prepare pro-forma income statements that basically forecast your financial performance over two to three years, using certain assumptions for investment capital.

Once you have completed a business plan that addresses your business and financial goals, it is time to take the plunge and manifest your dreams.

PART 2
The Execution Cycle

CHAPTER 5
Planning the Transition and Taking the Plunge

Transition is defined as "the act of passing from one state or place to the next or an event that results in a transformation." Going from being an employee to starting your own business is one type of transition. Having a business and looking to grow that business to a higher level of profitability, market penetration, or in a different direction is another type of transition.

In this chapter, I will cover how to prepare and complete the transition for three scenarios:

- Start-up of a new business;
- Growth of a current business using financial growth is a criteria;
- Growth of a current business by changing the product/service/ market focus of the company and essentially starting over again.

Start-up of a New Business

In making the transition from being an employee to starting your new business and getting it off the ground there are several things that you will need to do.

The first item on your "to do" list is to quit your current job. If you have no savings or means of additional income (like a spouse's income), then you should look at the option of starting your business on a part-time basis, if possible. Another option is to take unpaid leave which some large companies or government agencies will make available to their employees.

There are some major actions that need to be taken before you physically set-up your business. Some of these tasks can be done while you are still employed. Here is a sample of some of the items you should take care of in the order which they occur:

1. Choose your company name and logo.
2. Hire an accounting firm to help you structure your corporation and fiscal year to minimize tax and personal liability.
3. Set-up and complete the incorporation of your company.
4. Set-up business accounts for your company in the bank that you believe will be most supportive of your business venture over the long-haul.
5. Review your life and disability insurance needs with a reputable insurance provider and purchase the required insurance to protect your family and your income in the event of death or illness.
6. Make sure that you have an up-to-date will that has been prepared by a lawyer. It should include powers of attorney. This will be important should you be traveling and require your husband or some other trusted person to sign papers or be able to move money between business and personal accounts.
7. Determine where you are going to locate your business—your home, a shared office space, or a specific location with dedicated premises. If it is feasible to start your business out of your home, I would strongly recommend doing so. A business at home will minimize unnecessary expenses until you have brought in revenue. Many businesses can operate out of the home—usually those that are services-based.
8. Sign your lease with the land-lord of your office space and establish your business address.
9. Either print your own cards and stationary using publishing software, or engage a print shop to do that for you.
10. Hire a corporate lawyer/law firm you will use for tax, contract, and liability issues.
11. Purchase a dedicated computer for the exclusive use of your company.
12. Purchase Microsoft Office software, good anti-virus software, internet access, email capability, and back-up capability.
13. Purchase a versatile printer that can be used as a photocopier and can print large volumes of paper quickly.

14. Purchase a fax machine.

15. Purchase or commandeer office furniture that will be exclusively dedicated to your use.

16. Hire a part-time information technology consultant well-versed in pc software, hardware, and networks.

17. Set-up telecommunications infrastructure for your requirements— dedicated phone lines, mobile phone/blackberry, wireless local area network.

18. Meet with a corporate lawyer who specializes in employment, sub-contractor, and client contracts. Also, have the lawyer put together a non-disclosure agreement to protect the confidentiality of your company information when you have dealings with strategic partners/ joint-venture alliances and people who are outside of your company with whom you might have to share confidential information.

19. If you are not an accountant, hire a part-time book-keeper initially— once revenue starts to come in. Even if you are an accountant, weigh your time constraints and value-add to determine where your time is best spent.

20. If you have young children, hire a full-time nanny/housekeeper if you can afford it. Having your household chores and childcare responsibilities under control will allow you to focus on your business and keep your home organized and your family happy while you spend many hours at work.

21. If you can't afford a nanny, get yourself good, reliable daycare at the bare minimum. Don't delude yourself into thinking that you can run your business out of your home and keep an eye on the children. Don't bring your children to work, unless they are old enough to sit quietly and read, do homework, or help in some simple tasks within your business.

22. Get yourself a gym membership or set-up a simple home gym. Make the time to exercise regularly, preferably every day if at all possible. Even a daily thirty-minute walk will make a huge difference in centering you emotionally and creating a lot of additional physical energy. Remember, you are going to be working "crazy" hours until the business is generating income. You will get very fatigued. Exercise is one of the best ways to minimize your fatigue and the normal anxiety that goes along with tremendous change and uncertainty.

23. Make sure that you make time to enjoy your spouse, family, and good friends on a regular basis. With the flexibility of your business you may be able to drop off or pick up the kids from school a few days a week and spend some quality time with them running their errands and sitting with them while they do their homework. You might take breaks with them or just simply be physically near them doing your paperwork while they do their home work.

24. Getting a business off the ground can be a very lonely time—where you have to rely on yourself for a lot of things or must keep a lot of your uncertainty and worry to yourself. Keeping yourself healthy, psychologically speaking, involves the maintenance or cultivation of many personal relationships and an outlet to express your emotions and innermost thoughts.

Growth of Current Business-Financial Criteria

There is another very important type of transition I would like to discuss, and that is making the move to grow your company. Growth can happen many different ways. It can occur by growing:

- Revenue;
- Profit;
- Geography;
- Customer Base;
- Product or Service Offerings;
- Capital.

I will discuss each of these growth areas in more detail.

Revenue

Depending upon your industry and how your company is structured, revenue might be one of your most important indicators or metrics to demonstrate growth. Growth in revenue or sales signifies that you are growing your market share and allowing more capital to be mobilized by your company for a variety of reasons.

In order to be considered a major vendor or provider of product to your customer base, they may need to see that your sales or revenue base is growing.

Your bank may be looking for sales growth as an indicator of your long-term viability and as an indicator of your ability to service additional debt required for expansion.

You may have very specific goals regarding how much growth you would like to achieve in sales, year over year. This indicator might be your security blanket to really validate the long-term viability of your company in your own eyes. At the same time, you might be looking for additional sales to fund additional investment requirements of your business, like hiring additional sales people or augmenting your operations team.

Adding additional revenue might be as simple as working a little harder and a little smarter. It might also mean revising your business plan significantly. For example, to grow your company to the next level, you may want to get additional funding from the bank or venture capitalists. Of course, these two stakeholders will be looking for a solid growth trajectory in sales over the life of your company's history, as an indication of the future potential for sales growth.

Creating a plan that maximizes the likelihood of achieving your sales objectives each year, training your sales people so that they constantly grow and improve their performance, addressing the operations and customer fulfillment piece of your business so that it supports the sales process, will be extremely important.

You might need to explore innovations in your products or services, or alliances with other companies, to increase the likelihood of attracting new customers and new sales.

So the long and short of growing your revenue is that you have to set-out a business and sales plan, figure out what tools and support you will need to achieve these objectives, and then execute on your plan.

Profit

Profitability is another very useful way to make a growth transition for your company. The value of approaching profitability is that you may not have to grow your revenue—especially if you are in the middle of an economic downturn. By focusing on how you can increase your gross and net margins, you could potentially make much more money for small to negligible increases in revenue growth.

What do I mean by growing profitability? Well there are many ways to grow profitability. But the major thrust of this strategy is to reduce your costs, thereby increasing your margin.

There are many different ways of approaching cost reductions. You basically can look at improving costs with respect to people, process, or technology.

You can look at making your people more efficient, having them fulfill multiple roles or managing multiple projects simultaneously. This can be accomplished by hiring people with a very high-level of competency in your industry and by training them in time management and organizational skills, such as project management.

It can also be accomplished by reducing head-count and operating the same organization, but with fewer people. This can be a viable option, as long as people feel comfortable about their ability to handle additional responsibility and their compensation reflects this added scope. If people start leaving your company because they are burned out or feel over-worked, you may have created additional costs for your organization. This is because the cost of replacing these people and the disruption that their departure causes with respect to servicing customers may be more damaging in the long-run. Therefore, you must weigh this option very carefully.

The second area where you can squeeze additional cost reductions is with respect to processes used to create and fulfill customer orders, manufacturing, customer service, etc. By decreasing the time to complete a process cycle, you will be reducing your costs or speeding up the process to receive revenue. When you reduce costs or speed up the receipt of cash in your hands you automatically improve your profitability.

Another critical process that many companies are very poor at managing and that detrimentally affects cash flow, is speeding up payment by customers of accounts receivable. When you receive your money more quickly, you reduce your costs of financing your accounts receivable (line of credit). You also gain the stability and confidence to make investments when the timing is right rather than when the cash comes in.

Basically, the whole idea of process improvement is creating simpler and more predictable ways to run your business, which results in reducing your overall costs and improving your profitability.

The third area you can focus on to achieve cost reductions is through the use and leverage of technology. For example, if you currently have a store and do all of your sales through an adding machine, or perhaps you run a business that involves the management of significant volumes of inventory, technology can be used to speed-up customer transactions or to gain better control of your assets.

Technology, if it is used judiciously and properly, can help your business make dramatic breakthroughs. Take the blackberry for example; this invention has revolutionized the way people communicate with each other, book meetings, and keep contact information. Basically, you have a computer at your fingertips that can help you expedite meetings with customers, suppliers, or employees with the flick of your thumb— anywhere, anytime.

You should examine the internet and determine how you can best leverage this delivery channel to create alternate sources of revenue or cost reductions in the areas of customer service, recruitment, payments, and marketing.

The caveat with respect to technology is that you should be sure about its ability to speed up the receipt of revenue or improve your cost controls. Implementing technology should be kept as simple as possible, making small investments and measuring benefits immediately.

My own belief is that if the benefits are not demonstrable immediately, then you should not make the investment. Spending a lot of money on technology is a fallacy when you only see fuzzy benefits that have no real bearing on your bottom line. So beware and spend your money carefully in this area.

Geography

Another facet of growing your business is to look at geographical expansion. This expansion could be necessary in certain business sectors where, for example, high volumes of revenue and small profit margins require large customer bases.

You may also have a revolutionary product or service that is not available in any market. By bringing these products to market across your home-base country, or globally, you could be dramatically growing your business from many perspectives.

If you can demonstrate to your bankers or to investors that there are willing buyers in other markets, you could become the recipient of large sums of credit or investment. It is kind of like the chicken and egg of course, but if you receive funding, you will be able to hire employees in other countries to sell and deliver your products and services.

A lot of care will need to be exercised in how you invest this money since too much may drain your capital more quickly than the revenues received. But too little could hamper your ability to properly market, sell, and deliver high quality products as well.

Customer Base

Another approach to expanding your business to a greater level of success and achievement is increasing your customer base.

This expansion can be accomplished in two major ways:
1. Go deeper within existing markets; or
2. Diversify customer base by addressing several industry sectors.

If your business is focused on the consumer market you can increase your customer base by going after different segments of the same market. For example, if your business is targeted to working women, you may look at expanding your products and services to target young women. Cosmetics companies and spas are good examples of business ventures that address many segments of the same market.

For businesses focused upon commercial markets, the same principle applies. For example, in the IT systems integration industry, these companies frequently target different segments of the same customer. For example, if a particular bank is a customer, a systems integrator will traditionally go after the technology departments within a bank. In the process of trying to secure larger pieces of business within the same account, the systems integrator will target the business side of the bank to create additional demand for their services.

Most technology-based companies rely on this strategy to expand their customer base. IBM is a great case in point since virtually every part of a large commercial account will buy and use some of IBM's products or services.

The second approach in growing your customer base is to diversify the industry sectors in which you sell your products and services. Using the example of a retail business like a bakery, a customer base can be diversified by selling to consumers, grocery stores, coffee retail outlets (like Starbucks), catering to corporate customer events, and catering for weddings.

If we look at expanding the customer accounts of a software company that traditionally focused upon public sector accounts, a customer expansion strategy would be to market and sell product to other industries like utilities or financial service companies.

If the core competency of your company is marketing and sales and your product or service can address similar challenges across several industries, it is quite probable that your strategy will be successful.

Adding additional customers or markets is not only good for revenue it is also a great risk mitigation strategy. If one market declines, chances are the other market will be stable or even in growth mode. This is the principle of diversification of risk.

Product or Service Offerings

Your company has a portfolio of products and/or services that you offer to the market place to operate your business and make money. Another approach in creating growth for your business is to add new products or services to your current repertoire to attract additional revenue.

One of the benefits of being a privately-owned, entrepreneurial organization is that you can turn on a dime. The only caution you should take is not to spread your products so thinly that you dilute your focus and consequently fail at penetrating any market segment.

If you are running a retail business, for example, women's clothing and your specialty is business suits, you may decide to carry additional product lines like evening wear, or elegant casual wear. You may have noticed that business women only come in to your store at the beginning of each season, but that evening wear attracts women at all times of the year, but in the same income bracket as business women.

If you are running a service business focused upon the retail market such as a beauty salon, adding new services like a spa, or selling hair and nail products, or offering specialty services such as hair extensions or special events make-up can literally catapult your business to new sales heights.

On the commercial side, a consulting or accounting firm may be very successful in certain practice areas. By adding new practices that build upon the existing core competencies, new customers may be gained and of course new revenues that previously did not exist.

To determine whether new products or services are viable, it is important to do a market analysis like SWOT (strengths, weaknesses, opportunities, and threats) and prepare thorough financial projections of cost and sales. All your assumptions should be listed and vetted with key members of your management team, or a mentor who knows your industry. Adding new products and services is a no-brainer, once you have done the due diligence to determine the cost, benefit, and likelihood of success.

Capital

Expanding your business by increasing the capital available to you for investment in new people, R&D, technology, and process improvements is one of the most risky methods of growing your business to the next level.

If, for example, you decide that you want to go public at some time, be ready for a wild ride—the best of times, the worst of times. Even getting additional credit from the bank can be a double-edged sword.

I am not trying to paint a pessimistic picture, but the old adage that you don't get something for nothing, really applies in this case.

Yes capital is available. Yes, additional capital can catapult your business into the "big leagues." Yes, you will have to give up a significant degree of control to achieve this end if you proceed down this road. But proceed with caution.

If your company succeeds in growing and goes public, the sacrifices in giving up control over your company may well have been worth it. However, if your company does not meet its financial commitments to the VC's your fate might be like some good friends of mine who lost everything. All the investments these people made were lost when their VC's exercised their majority ownership and ousted them without any compensation whatsoever.

If you decide to get outside funding from VC's, make sure that you hire an excellent corporate lawyer who specializes in contracts with respect to funding from outsiders. Design your contract with an exit strategy in mind. Make sure that you borrow just enough money to give the company the boost it needs to capture new revenue.

Once you receive the funding, focus on a plan to achieve the sales and profit required to meet your commitments to the VC's. Make sure that you pay attention to operations issues, like putting in place financial and business controls, to ensure that there is no opportunity for wasting money or time.

Growth of Current Business—Re-Calibration

You might be in a situation where your business has grown as much as it can in its current state or with your current-level of capitalization.

You might be in a situation where your business is very successful, but you feel that you have stopped growing and are feeling stale and unmotivated. Alternatively, your business might be in decline, and to save the capital that you have built, it might be necessary to move the company into a completely new direction.

For people in these situations, it is time for re-calibration of your business—a change in direction.

A change in direction can result in new financial growth for your company. For others, new personal growth in the form of new business challenges or more time for personal interests is another outcome to be achieved by changing direction in your business.

For those who are at a difficult junction; that is, their business is on a holding pattern or even in decline, making a transition will be necessary for survival, if not growth.

The same principles that are used in getting a new business off the ground will apply to transforming an existing business, except that you will have some existing capital to leverage for the next stage.

Some of the major actions you will need to take to transform your existing business are:
- You will need to change your mind.
- To transform your business, the transformation must first start within you. You will need to let go of pre-conceived notions and assumptions that you have used to get you to this fork in the road. Using "new" eyes, it will be critical to do your personal inventory and market research to determine what your new focus will be.
- You will still need to do a business plan for the new product or service you plan to launch.

- You may need to dramatically trim down your business expenses, including laying off some employees.
- You will need to take another look at your financing provisions. Be sure to exercise a great deal of caution in taking on any new debt. For example, use debt to the extent that your existing revenue could pay down a loan or line of credit within 3-6 months.
- You should speak with your accountant about tax reduction strategies, including certain tax credits. You may also want to consider selling the existing business or incorporating a new company. Your accountant will be able to advise you on your options.

When you are at this stage in your business' life cycle, you are walking a fine line between preserving the financial assets you have now and building new assets and opportunities, potentially changing your whole business focus and strategy. In some ways, this situation is more difficult than starting a business from scratch, because there is a lot of psychological loss attributed to making a decision to wind-down a business that you have built up, but has plateaued, or worse is on the decline. At the same time, you may have revenue still coming in or long-term contracts in place. Therefore, you can't completely abandon ship. You must maintain what you currently have. Simultaneously, however, you will be fast-tracking the growth of your new venture or service offering. This whole exercise can make you feel more than a little schizophrenic.

So, constantly remind yourself to focus on the basics: sound marketing research, a solid business plan, strong sales and marketing execution, and tight cost management. You can be sure that you will encounter problems, challenges, and adversity, even at the best of times. How do you build the attitude, skills, and faith to get you through the challenging times that you will inevitably face?

CHAPTER 6
Managing Obstacles—Turning Adversity into Achievement

Well, well, so you want to be in business do you? You did your business plan. You got your business started. Everything is so new and exciting. You are on the right track. You are starting to see new revenue coming in and you are establishing some excellent relationships with new customers.

As you can imagine, not every day is a bed of roses. An entrepreneur's path is exciting, discouraging, euphoric, frustrating, and so "worth it," in the long run. The quote, "It was the best of times. It was the worst of times," sums it up perfectly.

To succeed in business, in anything for that matter, you will need to master the art of managing obstacles. There are many different types of obstacles you will encounter at the onset of launching your company or even running a successful business, day-to-day.

We will examine some of the typical obstacles that entrepreneurs face at every stage of a business' development. Your ability to turn problems into opportunities will have a direct impact on your ability to grow financially and professionally over the long-run.

Understanding the tactics and strategies in mastering the "battlefield of the mind" will help you to successfully navigate your way under, over, or through obstacles that come your way.

The typical types of obstacles you will encounter are external and internal.

Examples of external obstacles are:

1. **Not enough money to fuel your business strategy.**

This can be a tough one because money can always help to expedite getting your business operational. I am assuming in this scenario that you have exhausted your own savings. There are a number of ways that you can tackle this challenge.

One option is to build your business more slowly, focusing on generating short streams of revenue but enough to fund the development of your business in a staged fashion.

If you believe enough in your dream and are convinced of your ability to achieve it, you can approach friends and family for "angel" capital. If you use this approach, be certain to pay back every cent you borrow. Your reputation and relationships with people you care about are infinitely more important than money. However, many great companies got their start this way.

Your third option is to borrow money from the bank—which is often very difficult for new start-ups. A fourth option is to take out a second mortgage on your home or use credit lines or cards for start-up cash. You could also cash-out some investments or take your income tax refund and use these sources to get things started. Again, make sure that you have the ability to pay these debts back over a reasonable amount of time.

Another approach would be to secure venture capital funding, which is very difficult, even at the best of times. Be ready to give up a major share of your company and a great deal of autonomy, as well. This should be used as a last resort.

Expenses should be kept to the absolute minimum at this stage, which means working out of your home, printing your own business cards, bartering services to get things you need, and foregoing a salary until revenue starts to come in.

2. Lack of credibility or track record with customers.

How do you get new customers when you don't have a track record yet? The answer is imagination and perseverance. You need to become quite creative when you are facing an obstacle like this. The key is understanding what it will take to get your first client. Do you need to demonstrate your capability first—for example provide a sample for a customer to use in exchange for a reference or a referral?

Do you have previous customers you have worked with in your salaried position that you have developed strong personal relationships with? If so, they might be willing to write a recommendation or referral letter. They may have relationships with other potential clients in other similar organizations and can recommend you to some of their potential competitors, initially. For example, in the consulting or accounting services industry, a customer in one organization may know their counterpart in a competitive organization and have the power to recommend your company to their colleague, because there is no real competitive impact on their organization in doing so.

You might need to consider doing some pro-bono work in exchange for a customer reference. This customer reference represents money in the bank because when you have this base, other potential customers are willing to take a chance on you.

The other tactic you can use is to propose dramatic discounts to a prospective customer in exchange for them giving you a try on a small scale, buying a small order of products or giving you a small contract to provide services.

Another option is to use the tactic of leveraging your network. You may have excellent relationships with companies that service your target clientele but do not actually compete with you. This network could introduce you into your target client accounts, leveraging their existing relationships.

3. Inability to sell your product or service to address your sales objectives.

On this obstacle you need to determine if your selling skills are lacking or if your product/services are lacking, or if the market is just not open to your product/service at this time.

If your sales skills are not what they should be you need to get yourself up-to-speed as quickly as possible. There are many audio and video tape programs that can quickly teach you the basic building blocks of strong sales skills applicable to almost any industry. There are also numerous books you can make use of, specifically geared to the types of products and services that you will be selling.

If you have the financial means, your best bet would be to hire a strong, professional sales person. If that is not feasible, you could also engage a sales coach on an hourly basis to help you work through your major weaknesses.

If the issue is in fact that your products or services simply are not up to par with what your competitors are offering you need to know this fast. The easiest way to make this determination is to ask your prospective or current clients why they don't want to buy your products or services. Or you can ask them what it is about your competitors' products or services that they prefer over your own.

The internet is a great source of research. Many of your competitors have extensive web sites where they provide all kinds of information on their product or service marketing strategies.

Again, you may need to revisit your WOTS analysis and update it with your current findings. By understanding how your product is positioned from a weakness, opportunity, threat, and strength perspective, you might be able to re-calibrate your service offering or add new features to your products that would give them a competitive edge in the market place. You need to ask yourself what business or personal problem does my product or service solve? Who cares about this? What difference does it make? When you understand the answers to these questions, you will be better able to position your product from a marketing strategy point of view.

If the market is simply not ready for your product or service, by doing the foregoing analysis, you will be able to make this determination. You will probably need to re-visit your market research data. If you never did this analysis, maybe it is time to do it now. Following this analysis, you will be able to determine what the market needs at this time.

4. Not enough staff or the right mix of skills to support your business.

The right kind and mix of people to staff your business can be the difference between survival, growth, and death of your business.

First, you need to understand what positions and competencies are going to be critical to operate your business. The kinds of positions and competencies required will be determined by your industry and business model.

Prioritize the positions in your company based upon their ability to either generate sales or deliver products or services to customers. In general, sales roles are some of the most critical, since they have a direct bearing on your business' ability to bring in revenue.

To attract the right people, you will need to understand in detail what skills, competencies, and roles and responsibilities will be required for the job. A specific job description with a target salary range and a specific set of performance objectives is a mandatory requirement to communicate precisely what you need.

You can use the newspaper, the internet, job-search engines like monster.com and Workopolis, to recruit. Word-of-mouth, referral fees to existing employees who bring in new-hires, and head hunters are other means of attracting the right employees.

Understanding your industry, the human resource management practices such as compensation packages and retention strategies will allow you to at least match those of your industry. If people are particularly critical to your business, you may want to pay them a little more than the market average, to make sure that you retain the best people.

If you are operating in the commercial sector, other compensation alternatives such as bonuses based on sales revenue achieved, stock options, profit-sharing, planned sabbaticals, continuing education, tele-commuting (working at home part of the time) are all viable options to provide your potential employees.

Be very fussy about the people you hire. Don't compromise on your standards and values. Sometimes waiting to hire exactly the right person for the job is better than hiring a close facsimile.

Cultivate your intuition, especially when it comes to hiring the right people. If you feel any unease or discomfort during the interview, pay attention to these signals. If doubts pop up in your mind as you are interviewing or negotiating the "package" with the employee, again, pay attention. These are signals you are picking up about the person that are underneath the surface.

When you do references on the prospective employee, look for at least one reference that was a previous manager/boss, another reference that was a customer and a third reference that is either a subordinate or a colleague of the prospective employee.

If you do decide to make the employee an offer, make sure that you include a very specific probationary period, during which there will be specific objectives to be achieved. If those objectives are not achieved, it should be clearly communicated that employment will be terminated at that time. One of the hardest things that you can do is to fire someone. By keeping the conditions of employment quite specific, in terms of the role and responsibilities, objectives, and activities the employee will be responsible for, you will be able to determine if the employee is a keeper.

We will go into much more detail with regards to how to attract and keep the best employees in Chapter 7.

5. Poor customer service and inability to deliver products and services on time.

Whenever you have a problem honoring a commitment that you have made to a customer, you are eroding your credibility. The first step to take when this happens is to determine what the root cause of the problem is.

Frequent reasons for poor customer service and poor follow-through are:

- Over-committing to customers without checking with your delivery team on whether that deadline and service are reasonable. This also includes not communicating what the customer is expecting to your delivery team in a timely fashion.
- Not communicating delays to the customer in a timely fashion. Customers care most about honest and timely communication. No one likes to be surprised. By avoiding unpleasant communications, the problem actually becomes more annoying to the client.
- Not enough resources to handle the demand from customers, resulting in major delays or "screwed-up" orders.
- Broken processes are another major reason why companies can't deliver product or service to customers on time. If this is the case, walk through the process step-by-step and determine what parts don't work or don't add value to the final outcome. Once you have eliminated the non-value activities and have determined how best to streamline the whole process, document it and train or walk through

the process with your employees. Make sure they have mastered the improved processes and can put them into practice.

- Reliance on third party suppliers in order to deliver product or service to the customer. If you must rely on third parties, make sure that they are reliable and that they communicate with you in a timely fashion about any potential delays. If they are perpetually late or un-reliable, immediately find another supplier.

6. Poor money management, resulting in poor cash flow, spending money faster than you can make it, and bad credit ratings.

It is questionable as to whether this is an internal or external obstacle. It is actually a little bit of both. Poor cash flow can be due to many reasons: poor sales, slow turnaround on accounts receivable, and insufficient line of credit to cover slow accounts receivable.

If poor sales are the reason for your poor cash flow, you need to immediately look at ways to beef up your sales. If it is a question of effort and focus, put some elbow grease into it. If there other issues such as poor market adoption of your product, you are looking at a product positioning problem, not a sales problem.

If your accounts receivable are taking too long to collect, focus more energy on collecting them. Get someone or do it yourself if need be. Call your customer and very politely insist on getting paid. Offer to pick up the cheque if need be. Explain how important it is for you to be paid on time. Help them to understand that not being paid on time compromises your business and your ability to pay your employees on time.

If your line of credit is insufficient, you must approach your bank for more help. You may have to sign a personal guarantee or put a lien on your home to get a sizeable line of credit.

Another option is to time your payments with your accounts receivable. You might be able to pay employees as contractors and compensate them on a monthly basis instead of on a bi-weekly basis.

If overspending is your problem, you are in major trouble. Most people's assumption when they overspend is that cash will continually come in to keep paying the bills. You might be very lucky for awhile, but eventually the normal business cycles that affect every business will affect yours. Inevitably, your business will slow down in response to economics or changes in customer behavior, or a host of other reasons. When that happens, overspending, that is using more cash than you have or leaving little cash reserves or capital in your business will become your greatest obstacle to success.

For businesses that are successful, overspending is often the single reason that companies like these go belly up. Calculate how much you need to run your business and what kind of reserves you need to keep it properly capitalized. Any cash above this level can be used for spending. But again, be careful; you still need to establish personal reserves in addition to those that you have established for your business. I would advise no less than one year's salary to be set aside for an emergency, at the very least. Any cash you have over and above should be spent with pleasure, but you should put away at least 10% or more for investment purposes, as well. Again, we will get into more details about good financial management in Chapter 8.

7. Too much work coupled with too many responsibilities or instability at home.

Women who do too much—women entrepreneurs? Do we have a genetic predisposition for the disease to please? Yes, yes, and yes!

How do you work against your natural inclinations, especially those that feel so right, like doing everything and doing it perfectly? The answer is, learn to prioritize and delegate.

What are your priorities? How does your family rank up there with your ambition and desire to achieve your goals? No one can tell you what to focus on or where to place more of your energy. What everyone can agree upon, however, is the need for balance in all aspects of your life. If your family is happy and healthy, chances are, you will be better able to focus upon your business and vice-versa.

If you are trying to do everything at home and are trying to do everything at work, everything will suffer, especially you. I recently came across the case of a smart and successful CEO who runs a major beverage manufacturing company. Her responsibilities in the business were considerable. Her responsibilities at home were considerable as well. She had a very ill member of her family to take care of. She refused to get nursing care or housekeeping assistance. She insisted on caring for her ill family member herself and sharing house-keeping duties for her 8,000 square foot mansion with her children.

Ask yourself, how could any member of her family, benefit from her inability to delegate any of her responsibilities? Money was not the issue. Her inability to trust others with the delegation of her responsibilities was the root of the problem. Her health suffered, she looked haggard and was exhausted all the time. Ultimately she could not give the best of herself to her business or her family. The result was lose-lose all around, especially for her.

Make sure to delegate responsibilities at home if you have a heavy load in your business. For example, get help with the housework, cooking, and child care. Hire permanent or temporary help in these areas. If you can afford it, hire a full-time nanny/cook/housekeeper. You will be able to come home and enjoy your children and have the energy to play with them and give them your all. You can't do that if you are coming home from the office late, rushing to fix dinner, cleaning the house.

What about your spouse or partner? Doesn't he deserve a relaxed and happy wife who is fulfilled by her family and her business? When you focus your energy on the things that count, the effect of your focus multiplies. Your husband becomes happier and more supportive. Your children become well-adjusted and feel secure. Your business gets your undivided attention when you are there. Win, win, and win. This is the name of the game.

Don't be a martyr. Don't be a saint. Just be a happy, fulfilled woman who loves herself and her family so much that she organizes her time where it best serves everyone's interests, including her own.

Internal obstacles are to be found in the " battlefield" of the mind. These are the most difficult obstacles to overcome. This is because the war that must be won is that with your psyche. Our perceptions can help or hinder us. The problem is that we don't necessarily digest these perceptions the way we should. That is, we believe our perceptions, especially negative ones, and end up actualizing our worst fears.

Some examples of our internal obstacles are discussed in points 8 through 14.

8. You get too easily discouraged, resulting in unreasonable worry or intermittent depression.

Everything comes in cycles. We have cycles of excitement, hope, and motivation. Unfortunately, we also experience cycles of disappointment, setbacks, and uncertainty.

Owning your own business is a journey of faith: faith in yourself, faith in your customers, faith in your employees, and faith in God.

Earlier, I mentioned that optimism is the entrepreneur's secret weapon. That has definitely been my experience. As I researched the lives and strategies of successful entrepreneurs, I discovered that I am not alone in this belief.

Getting discouraged or worried is a normal part of the process of living. Of course, running your own business makes you more likely to feel attached to the outcome of everything that touches your business' success.

Keeping your optimism alive is sometimes very difficult. It can be very easy to give in to worry and discouragement. When this happens it is very important to know how to put things into perspective and regenerate your enthusiasm and drive.

Here is an approach I like to use when I start drowning in worry. I basically work on re-programming my thoughts by remembering an acronym I have, called PUNCH. PUNCH taps into my natural instincts to fight for myself and my family by taking care of "business."

P—Is for ponder and pray. I like to take some time to be on my own and to be quiet with my thoughts. I break down the problem into bite-size pieces. I try to understand whether I am facing a real problem or simply my perceptions. Sometimes, I imagine worries that are not based upon anything real. After I have pondered the problem and broken it down into pieces I can work with, I pray. If you don't believe in prayer, then simply meditate. Empty your mind and allow yourself to be open to the insights or solutions that float into your mind.

U—Is for understand. During my prayer and meditation, I start to understand what the root of my problem really is and the possible alternative solutions that are available to me. As I start to understand myself and the potential solutions to my problem, my sense of optimism and energy or drive starts to take over the negative emotions.

N—Is for nuke the negativity. Once I understand the root of my negativity and worry, I visualize annihilating it, blowing it up, that is, nuking it. This visualization is very powerful and gets my creative and warrior juices flowing again.

C—Is for choice, as in taking concrete action to move forward with my chosen solution. The biggest antidote to worry is action. Not any action will do, of course. That is why the pondering and prayer are extremely important. They allow my intuition to be tapped into, which always reveals my best choices for a positive solution.

H—Stands for hammer. I am the hammer and every worry or problem is a nail. My job is to take action and hammer out a solution to the crisis at hand.

I use **PUNCH** to literally punch my way out of any battle, real or perceived. Don't stay stuck or paralyzed by worry or fear. Use tools like the ones I have described to create a habit of fighting problems in a healthy way that honors your intuition and allows you to discern the real from the imagined.

The other issue I haven't covered is depression. It is a serious issue and should not be underestimated. If you feel that your worry and feelings of discouragement are becoming frequent and that you feel down more than any other emotion, it is time to take action of a different sort. Go see your doctor. Understand what is at the bottom of your depression. If you feel that you can sort through these emotions by speaking with a psycho-therapist—great, do it. However, if there are other things behind your depression like health issues, you need to take action right away. Depression is an insidious disease. It affects anyone from any walk of life. Sometimes you can't just "tough" it out. Sometimes you have to deal with this issue medically.

In addition to medicine, exercise, a nutritional diet, eliminating addictions like alcohol, drugs, or spending can be instrumental in combating depression.

Remember, the sooner you deal with a problem like depression in an effective manner, the sooner your life will be under control. You will be able to face problems calmly and with strength. You will be able to bounce back from disappointments.

Make sure that throughout a crisis like this, you learn to gather support and talk to people who can help you by listening and by offering useful advice and action-oriented help.

9. You feel that the weight of the world is on your shoulders, but there is no one to share the burden.

Whether you are the CEO of Microsoft or the CEO of Mom and Pop Inc., your path can be a very lonely one. Many times you will want to share a concern or fear with the people you work with or even your husband, but you must keep it to yourself. You keep it to yourself for many reasons. You don't want to be perceived as weak. You don't want to create anxiety and worry in the people who work for you.

Incidentally, many successful CEO's end up imploding, when they adhere to the "strong-silent" approach.

It is dangerous and unhealthy to keep all your concerns and worries to yourself. The thing that most women need to learn is what they should share and when it is appropriate to do so.

First, your husband should be a logical choice to share your ups and downs with. Of course, we can't assume that all husbands are supportive in all instances. For those husbands/partners who have difficulty with challenges and stress, it can sometimes be more draining for you to share these things with him, because he feels powerless to help you. In the end, you may end up comforting and re-assuring him more than getting the support that you need.

In this type of situation, you need to have a good back-up support like a good and loyal friend. Sometimes a good friend can be more nourishing to your soul than an actual family member.

Remember my earlier advice about developing relationships with mentors and coaches? If you have these people already assembled, now is exactly the time that you need their strength and sage advice.

If you do not have someone you can go to who has the experience and wisdom to counsel you with respect to your business, the next possible alternative is a good and trusted friend. Keep in mind that your friend may not have the required experience to advise you. However, sometimes just having someone you can talk to, and who can just sit and listen to you vent is enough to keep you on track.

If you have specific concerns that need to be addressed with your staff, then it is important that you have the level of comfort and control to talk to them about the problem. If you need their support or a change in behavior, you need to be clear about the changes that need to happen and the timeframe for these actions.

10. You take rejection personally and let it affect your level of motivation.

The first thing you must remember is that the rejection you receive in the business world is very rarely personal. As such, you need to move past rejection into the realm of analysis and action.

When we are rejected in business, that is, we don't get the order, or a prospective client tells us they don't want to meet us or do business with us, we need to understand what the real issue is. Rejection is an opportunity for learning and improvement. Sometimes rejection becomes the seeds with which greatness is sown. Let me give you the perfect example I came across the other day. I read a short anecdote about Mahatma Gandhi. Gandhi originally lived in South Africa, and as with most African countries, not to mention the U.S. in the early part of the century; segregation and racial bigotry were rampant. One day, Gandhi got thrown off a train, simply because of the color of his skin. They say that when Gandhi was thrown off this train in South Africa, he closed his eyes and saw the British Empire crumbling halfway across the world. Gandhi's rejection experience would change the course of history and create an independent India.

So the point of my story, of course, is that rejection is a powerful transformation opportunity. Stop and analyze why you have been rejected. Is it because of the way you communicate? Do you clearly understand your value proposition and differentiators? Do you honor your commitments? Are you talking to the right person—a decision-maker? Are you interacting with enough customers?

Basically, you can use the same approach I described previously, called PUNCH, to discern what you can learn from the rejection and how to take action to hammer out a solution.

11. You are afraid to hurt other people's feelings or address conflict in a healthy fashion.

For many women, dealing with conflict is a major challenge. By and large women either try to be overly accommodating and nurturing of people or situations that don't meet their expectations or they act the part of the bitch, ranting and railing at the source of their displeasure.

There really is a happy medium between these two extremes. The trick is to focus on specific outcomes that need to happen or be achieved by an employee or even a customer. By focusing on outcomes, you can start to gain clarity and objectivity in dealing with an employee who is not performing. The same goes with a customer. Sometimes customers ask us to perform the impossible and then don't fulfill their end of the bargain by signing contracts or making commitments in a timely manner.

Focus on the outcomes or performance objectives. If your problem is with your employee, schedule regular review sessions to assess the employee's effectiveness in meeting his or her performance goals. If they are not meeting these goals, voice your concern, even your disappointment. But, try to work with the employee to determine next steps and actions required to get them on track. If the employee consistently fails to redress the situation, then take action with them.

Either put the employee on probation or fire her or him. Don't make excuses for her or him or coddle her or him, because contrary to your intentions of being kind, the employee will perceive you as being weak or worse, as someone that can be easily manipulated.

If you have conflicts with a customer, you can be polite and respectful. But, you must clearly address the problem you have and recommend a solution to address it. Always negotiate a compromise. Never issue ultimatums; they are always ineffective, no matter how much you are in the right. Remember, when you negotiate win-win agreements, you are preserving the relationship in the long-term.

12. You are afraid of making the wrong decision, so you avoid making any decisions.

Ah, the dreaded "P" word, procrastination. They should rename procrastination and call it paralysis. Something is very unpleasant to you, so you keep putting it off until you can't put it off anymore. Usually, by the time you have decided to take action on the issue, you have taken several years off your life, worried yourself to death, or blown up the problem into mythic proportions.

There is a wonderful technique you can use to help minimize procrastination. Either the night before or first thing in the morning, you should make a list of all of the things that need to get done. Attack the biggest, hairiest "to do" first and get it out of the way. You will notice an interesting phenomenon. You will achieve 80% of your business' success by doing 20% of the critical things that need to get done.

Good examples of this phenomenon are cold calling and prospecting; meeting and dealing with customers, even the difficult ones; reviewing key employee's performance with them on a regular basis; and addressing customer complaints or problems.

13. You think you are always right and have difficulty listening to opinions that don't jive with your own.

One of the blessings and curses of the entrepreneur is that you have faith in yourself and your decisions. Sometimes this faith and confidence can be to your detriment. If you don't listen to other people's opinions, especially those that contradict your own, you are in serious trouble.

Remember the earlier discussion around rejection? The same goes for your listening skills. Sometimes the greatest breakthroughs and opportunities arise when employees feel confident in giving you honest feedback with respect to improvement opportunities.

There are some cardinal principles of listening and communication.

Create an environment where people feel safe and comfortable about sharing honest feedback on any business-relevant topic in the work place.

Allow people to speak freely in either a public forum in your business or privately with you in your office, behind closed doors.

Always allow people to make their views heard without any interruptions.

Don't interrupt, don't interject, and don't gesture or grimace, at all. Look people straight in the eye. Keep an open posture and positive body language. Nod or acknowledge what the other person is telling you.

Reflect back the information you understood from the "messenger.

Repeat what you heard and understood. Ask the person if you understood correctly. If they confirm that your understanding is correct, then acknowledge your appreciation of the person's insights or opinions.

Provide your honest feedback on the person's recommendations.

If the topic of conversation is complex and you disagree with the employee, request additional time to think through the issue or request. Let your employee know that you need time to think about this and that you will get back to them within a short, but reasonable time frame.

Take the time to think about the issue.

Discuss it with other people who have the expertise and knowledge to shed some light on the subject. You may not want to reveal who the source of the information is, especially if they have requested confidentiality.

Get back to the person with your decision.

If it is possible to give them what they need or to allow them to implement a new idea, then by all means do so. If you do not agree with their opinion or recommendation, tell them so. Dispassionately explain your rationale to them, especially if it is a touchy subject. If it is possible to offer some compromise on a few of the points that will create good will or will motivate your employee, then do so. If it is not possible, explain why. At the end of the discussion, commend your employee on their insights or their loyalty or creativity. The point here is making them feel that their viewpoint and intellect is sincerely appreciated and respected.

Encourage open, honest communications with employees and customers. Sometimes being right is not always the best-case scenario. Sometimes you will need to give a little to get a little. The caveat to this condition is if employees suggest something illegal, unethical, or will pose unreasonable risk to your business. In this case, shut them down immediately. You might need to consider firing them in this particular scenario, especially if they are advocating something illegal or unethical.

The main message of these communication principles is that everyone's opinion must be respected, and that every employee should feel safe about providing honest and real opinions. The last thing you should ever want is a bunch of "yes" men or women around you. This is bad news to the long-term viability of your business.

14. You are always extremely busy, but not productive.

Productivity is still the major obstacle that most executives cite as limiting their effectiveness. Time is probably the most precious resource you will ever need. Do you use your time wisely?

Are you busy, but not with anything that helps you generate the majority of your revenue or customer success stories?

Remember the infamous 80/20 Rule? Eighty percent of your productivity or value to any activity comes from twenty percent of your efforts. The corollary applies as well. Only twenty percent of your value comes from eighty percent of your work-effort. What does this rule teach us? It teaches us that our unique value and knowledge is what drives our productivity and success.

If you focus most of your time and efforts on what you are uniquely good at and what brings you success, your habits become a self-fulfilling prophecy. The opposite is true as well. If you waste your time on busy and urgent tasks, but these activities are not tied to selling, building relationships with customers, mentoring key employees, or managing your cash-flow, your time and energy will be wasted.

Given the enormous amount of information out there on time management, I will confine myself to the principles of productivity that I and other very successful people use to guide how we spend our time.

Take the time to plan your day, week, and month.

Set aside some time to plan your activities for each day. Usually the best time to do this is the night before—either before you leave the office or while you are in bed before you go to sleep. The same principle applies to planning your week and month. Instead of focusing just on a "to do" list, instead create a set of goals you intend to achieve.

- Set 3 goals for each day. For example, the types of goals you want to set each day should be related to making contact or meeting with a key client, resolving a major human resources issue, or reviewing progress status of your sales team.
- Set 5 goals each week. For example, the types of goals you will set each week might revolve around getting a decision from a client on whether or not they are going to buy your products or services, getting a major contract signed, hiring a key employee, or opening a new account.
- Set 10 goals each month. These goals will be at a slightly higher level, such as sign contracts or close sales for $100K in the following key accounts, create new opportunities or orders from new prospects, or review sales team progress and performance and achieve monthly sales goal.

Your goals are very much tied into your business plan. They are the details of how you will implement your business plan on a daily, weekly, and monthly basis.

Another item tied into your time-boxed goals are the reports you will need to manage your business. For example, the typical types of reports that you will use to manage your business are monthly and year-to-date income statements, cash-flow statements including status of all current bank accounts, line-of-credit report for your bank, sales report—monthly and year-to-date, gross margin reports, and weekly activity status reports for your sales and customer service organizations.

Be Hard-hearted with Time Interrupters

I classify time interrupters as any person or thing that prevents me from operating at my highest level of effectiveness. Your effectiveness is ultimately measured by how much revenue or profit you nurture and build for your company each day.

The typical time interrupters can be described as:
- people who constantly interrupt you for non-critical issues;
- people who are not capable of fulfilling their duties and responsibilities but constantly need your help.
- phone calls that don't generate revenue; and
- email and correspondence that does not relate to closing business, serving customers, or supporting your front-line employees.

People Interrupters

There are lots of well-meaning employees who will constantly interrupt you for "urgent," but non-critical issues. Your task is to limit these interruptions as much as possible. You can do this by designating one hour or time period each day where people can drop by or, better yet, schedule time to get your signature on paper work, or time to get your input with respect to different decisions that need to be made.

When you don't want to be interrupted, close your door and communicate to your assistant that no one is to interrupt you, unless there is a real emergency. Sometimes, I escape to my home office to work on a proposal for a customer and can count on no interruptions whatsoever. The benefit to me is that this proposal would take all day to complete at the office, in between various interruptions, versus completing it in a couple of hours at home. With the remaining hours in the day, I can go back to the office and deal with other important issues like calling clients or liaising with employees. Each task receives the focus and attention that it deserves.

The other type of people interrupter is the employee who needs your help with respect to making a decision on a client issue or getting your input with respect to a sales or customer service approach. This kind of interruption is ok and healthy when the employee learns from the experience and goes on to solve similar problems without your input at every turn. The problem becomes evident when the employee comes back to you again and again with the same types of issues, questions, or problems and doesn't seem to be able to learn from previous experience and to apply it.

If the latter scenario is the one you are dealing with frequently, you need to review the employee's progress with them on a regular basis. Make sure that you establish a probationary period up front with the employee and stick to it. If the employee can't seem to evolve or improve and you see the same behavior repeating itself, and the probationary period is at an end, it is time to terminate the business relationship, as difficult as that might be.

Phone Calls and Email Interrupters

These are the most insidious interrupters because they are constant and addictive. Anyone who owns a Blackberry knows how addictive it can be to hear the device buzzing with a new email, and compulsively needing to check the device to see what has arrived.

The same thing applies to receiving calls on your cell or land line or receiving an email on your PC while you are working on a document at your desk. With these interrupters, you need to establish some rules as to how and when you will answer calls and emails.

I use the following general rules. If a call comes in and I am in a meeting, I don't answer the phone. I let voice mail step in. If I am driving and a call comes in, I will decide whether I should answer the call. I generally don't like to speak on my cell when I am driving. When I do, I use an earpiece to keep my hands free. If I am busy working on a proposal or an email to a customer, I don't answer any calls, unless they are from customers.

When I receive email while working at my desk, I will intermittently check to see if anything has been received that is client—or account-management related. If it is nothing urgent I will wait to respond.

For setting up meetings, I make use of Microsoft Outlook. When I don't have the flexibility to schedule meetings myself, I ask clients to connect with my assistant, who has access to my calendar and can schedule the meetings for me.

The basic message I have to communicate to you is use every moment wisely. Leverage your unique strengths and invest most of your time and energy in these assets. Remember the unique qualities that make you an individual are the reason you have started or methodically grown your business.

Adversity, problems, doubts, and crises are inevitable things we all have to deal with in the game of life. For an entrepreneur, obstacles are like weight training for your muscles. The more you learn to overcome obstacles and deal with them in a healthy manner, the stronger you get mentally, spiritually, and physically.

CHAPTER 7
Mastering Solution Selling

Selling is a powerful, difficult, and necessary part of every company's growth and success. The products and services you sell, as well as your target markets will determine the type and extent of your sales approach. For the purposes of this chapter, I will cover the fundamentals of solution selling that addresses both tactical and strategic selling skills.

If you are not a seasoned sales professional, I would strongly recommend that you take a course in strategic or solution selling, in addition to reading this chapter. It will be necessary for you to master all of the mechanics of selling before you can get into selling or lead your newly established company's sales team. I cannot emphasize enough how important the mastery of sales skills is. It will make the difference between becoming a self-made millionaire and just simply getting by.

Unfortunately, the statistics with regards to the financial performance of women-owned businesses don't tell a very good story about financial performance and growth. Mastering sales skills and teaching your key employees how to master these skills will make a huge difference in turning your company into a financial powerhouse. Remember, not all pieces of the solution-selling process will be relevant to your business. However, even if you learn one or two valuable skills in managing the sales of your business from this chapter, it will have been worthwhile.

This chapter will cover the critical pieces of the solution-selling process from both the tactical and strategic perspectives. The components of the solution-selling process that we will cover are:

- The sales preparation and initiation cycle:
- How to do a sales plan;
- How to develop sales materials and tools;
- How to cold call;
- The sales execution cycle:
- How to conduct and follow up sales calls with customers;

- How to qualify opportunities;
- How to respond to Request for Proposals or Request for Quotes;
- How to manage prospect accounts;
- How to manage activity and performance;
- How to close deals; and
- How to manage customer accounts.

Sales Preparation and Initiation

The sales preparation and initiation process is all about getting your ducks in a row so that you can be productive and focused once you get going on selling to your customer.

How to do a Sales Plan

Remember your business plan? Well your sales plan is basically taking your business plan to the next level of detail to document how you will go about getting sales for your new product or service.

Your sales plan is quite simple. It contains your sales objectives for the fiscal year, broken down by product or service and by the customer or customer segment that you will be selling to. Keep it simple. You don't need to write reams of paper to make your sales plan useful. Put it in point form and use a tool like Microsoft PowerPoint to document the following pieces of your sales plan:

1. Sales objectives by sales person and/or product or service for a particular market segment.

Example—

Sales Revenue Objectives for Mary-Ann Massad for fiscal 2006/07: $5 million, total revenue

Program/Project Management Services: $2 million

Process Improvement Services: $1 million

Motivational Speaking and Media Sales: $2 million

Revenue targets by Customer Segments:

Financial Services: $2 million

Government: $1 million

Consumer: $2 million

2. Product and Services Description
3. A SWOT Analysis (Strengths, Weaknesses, Opportunities, Threats)
4. An action plan regarding how you will sell your products and services to those accounts.
5. A description of the tools, resources, and research you will require to support your activities.

How to develop Sales Materials and Tools

To sell your products and services, you will need sales or marketing tools to communicate your capabilities to customers. You can make use of the following types of marketing materials to support you and your team in your sales efforts:

- Marketing brochures and presentations;
- Web site with e-commerce capability if you want to sell any products or services directly from your web site.
- A telephone script for cold calls;
- Documented Reference Stories or Customer Testimonials; and
- Letter or Email of introduction to summarize why your prospective client should meet with you.

These tools will be used at different points in the sales cycle to either provide introductory information or more in-depth information to substantiate why a customer should meet with you or refer you to other people in their organization.

How to Cold Call

Cold calling is the most daunting part of selling. It can be arduous, frustrating, and can take a long time to reach customers and book meetings with them.

There are some strategies to make cold calls more manageable and likely to result in booking a meeting with your customer.

First, do your research on your customer account or segment before you start calling on anyone. Understand the issues and challenges that your customers are facing. Is there a clear relationship between a potential customer's challenge and the product or service you want to provide them with? That is, can your product fill an un-tapped need or improve your customer's productivity?

You need to be able to clearly articulate your understanding of your client's business and how your product or service can help them or demonstrate how you have been able to help their competitors.

You should develop a telephone script for yourself addressing your differentiation message, how you will handle different objections, and asking for the appointment or meeting.

You should also have your introductory letter or email and any other marketing materials ready, so that if your customer asks you to send the information as a prerequisite to booking the meeting, you will have it ready to go.

The principles of a powerful differentiation go something like this:

Good morning, Mr. Customer, my name is Mary-Ann Massad. I am a Managing Partner with Knowsys Group here in Toronto. Knowsys Group is a strategic IT management consulting firm that specializes in managing large-scale programs on time and budget, and process improvement for technology-based organizations—reducing costs and improving service levels to customers. The purpose of my call is to request a meeting with you over the next couple of weeks, to discuss how Knowsys Group has helped bank A, B, and C, successfully manage enterprise-wide IT programs in the $10 to 100 million range. I would like to share our capabilities with you and also better understand your key objectives, initiatives, and challenges, so we can establish a business relationship with your organization.

If you break down the message the components of it are as follows:
1. Greet the customer and introduce yourself.
2. Very briefly describe your services.
3. Link your services to other organizations like theirs and how you have been able to help their competitors solve a particular problem or address a particular need.
4. Request a meeting with the client during a particular time-frame, within a two-week or month period or suggest some specific dates when you are available.
5. Summarize the proposed agenda of your meeting with the customer.
6. Offer to send the client some background material so that they will be briefed as to your capabilities before the meeting.

Your cold calls don't just have to be conducted on the phone. They can also be done through email. I find that many of my customers hate using their phone and sifting through voice mail. Instead, they constantly read their Blackberry emails and tend to respond to them right away. If this is the culture of your target customers, then I suggest that you supplement a call to these clients with follow-up emails requesting a meeting.

If you have the ability to warm up a cold call by referring to an article you have read about the prospect, or perhaps an acquaintance that you have in common, or better yet, a colleague of the prospect who has referred you to the prospect—even better. The point here is try to find something or someone in common with the prospect, so that she feels more comfortable about meeting with you.

You can make use of tools like Microsoft Outlook or their new sales management tool, Salesforce.com, ACT, or Goldmine to manage all of your sales calls. You basically want to have a tracking tool that allows you to see who you have called, all of their particulars (phone, email, address, etc.), the outcome or follow-up required. In this way, you can see when prospects or clients must be followed up with and what you have committed to them.

This type of report becomes the major tool you will use to manage your sales activity.

You should have a good understanding of how many clients you will need to meet with to create a solid, qualified opportunity. Depending on the standards of your industry, you will need to book a lot of meetings to create the number of opportunities required to generate a certain level of revenue.

I would say that a general rule of thumb is you should see a minimum of two prospects or clients each day (on average). In some industries, this level of activity might be insufficient. Therefore, it is important to understand the practices and sales activity benchmarks of your industry if you want to be a leader.

Sales-Execution Cycle

The sales-execution cycle is all about getting in front of the client, building a relationship, closing the sale, and providing continuous service to the customer, in order to create repeat business and references.

How to Conduct Sales Calls

There are some fundamental principles to conducting successful sales calls. These principles are centered on good communication. That means that, as a rule, you should spend as much of your time with the client as necessary asking questions to get information and intelligence on their objectives, problems, challenges, frustrations, and success stories with other vendors (perhaps competitors of yours). Your questions should be as open-ended as possible, in order to allow the customer an opportunity to share their thoughts, perspectives, and knowledge of the business with you.

Close-ended questions with a response of yes or no are usually useful for qualifying or closing the sale.

You will need to spend a certain amount of time communicating your capabilities to your prospect or customer. To keep this information, short, sweet, and relevant, you should structure the presentation on the OBF method. The OBF method stands for Objectives, Benefits, and Features.

When you communicate objectives, in the OBF method, you are focusing on what the client's objectives are. The objectives may be industry-standard objectives for clients in your industry or they might be specific to the prospect/client in question, based on research that you have done or based on previous information-gathering meetings you have had with the customer. Examples of objectives are things like: your prospect wants to reduce their costs by x% or improve their order fulfillment cycle time by y%.

The benefits in the OBF method are the proven benefits of the products or services you are selling. Benefits are the results or performance enhancements that your product or service will deliver. Examples of benefits are things like decreasing the client's operational costs, or speeding up the cycle for manufacturing of products, resulting in faster order fulfillment, which means that revenue will come into the client's organization more quickly.

The features in the OBF method are the characteristics of your products or services. Hopefully, these characteristics are unique compared to your competitor's offerings. But the main thing to remember here is that the features of your product are much less important than the client's objectives you are trying to address and even less important than the benefits that your product will deliver.

When you focus on these three elements, spending at least two-thirds of your time on the objectives and benefits, and only one-third of your time on the features, the prospective client gets a clear message about how you can help her.

Throughout your presentation of the objectives, benefits, and features, you should be asking questions like: is this objective accurate and does it reflect your situation? Is this benefit important to your organization? If not, what benefit would be of greater importance? Which of these features differentiates our product or service in your opinion, Mr./Ms. Client?

By constantly asking questions of the client, you allow them to voice any concerns or objections—openly. When you understand what a client's objection or concern is, you have an opportunity to demonstrate how your product or service could help your client.

If you don't know what the client's objections are, you will have little or no opportunity to close your sale.

How to Qualify Opportunities

Part of your questioning process should center around qualification of the client and the opportunity. For example, basic questions you should ask the client are:

- What is the decision-making process for this type of investment?
- Who are some of the other stakeholders that will need to be involved in this decision?
- Do you have the budget and authority to make a buying decision?
- If not, who does?
- Are there other vendors you are considering for this opportunity?
- What is your timeframe to make a decision?
- What kinds of benefits would make it easier to cost-justify an investment of this nature?
- What steps will need to be taken for you to purchase this product or service?

Qualification questions are extremely important because they can provide you with the information you need to close the sale. Without this information, you will not have the intelligence to figure out what other tactics and actions are necessary to close the deal.

The best opportunities are those you have shaped from scratch, based upon an un-fulfilled need or unsolved problem the client has. Here, your chances are almost 90% or better for winning the opportunity, especially if you are dealing with the decision-maker and she has the budget to pay for the product or service.

If you are responding to a specific need or requirement that the client has spent a lot of time thinking through, then you might still be behind the "eight-ball." The chances are that your competitors have already been discussing the requirement and shaping the client's perceptions and opinions on their ability to address their needs. If this is the case, you will have a lot of catch-up to do.

How to Respond to Request for Proposals

Customers frequently make large purchasing decisions through the use of request for proposals (RFP's) or request for quotes (RFQ's) or request for information (RFI's). Responding to a request for proposal is often expensive and takes a significant amount of time and effort. However, responding is worthwhile when you have either worked with the client previously or have been actively involved in educating the client about your products or services, so that your unique features or benefits become the basis for the RFP.

Responding to an RFP without intimately knowing the client and her requirements, as well as having shaped the opportunity, is not advised. Even when you have helped to shape the opportunity, you still might lose. If you are responding "blind," that is, you have never dealt with this client before, your chances of winning are slim to none.

How to Manage Prospect Accounts

Your objective in managing prospect accounts (those that have not become customers yet) is to understand the prospect(s) and their organization intimately. This means that you should be constantly scanning newspapers, magazines, and the internet for information. The more you know about their plans, strengths, achievements, weaknesses, challenges, and competitors, the better positioned you will be to close a sale.

If you are selling to a company, obtaining an organization chart is critical. An organization chart is a map of the key decision-makers, influencers, and recommenders. Your job is to get to know everyone who might play a possible role in the sale of your product or service.

If you want to build a strong, long-term relationship with this prospect, and turn her into an excellent customer, then you must be visible within the account at all times. Whether it is meeting with key people or inviting others to presentations, conferences, workshops, or social events, you and your company must be constantly visible to their organization.

To make sure that you are calling on these prospects in a timely manner (not bothering them but still staying on their radar screen), use your sales tools like your call history sheets to assess when you should be calling to follow up with your prospects.

How to Manage Activity and Performance

Whether you are managing your own activity and results, or those of your sales team, you can take advantage of a couple of key reports that will help you understand what steps you need to take to achieve your sales goals.

One of the most basic tools you can use is a calendar to view your planned meetings, as well as those meetings you have conducted in the past. The calendar of meetings will tell you if you have enough activity to create the pipeline of opportunities in the first place. Sometimes, it might seem like you are very busy, but by observing the historical level of activity required to bring in a sale, you will be able to assess whether or not you and/or your team need to pump up the volume in order to achieve a baseline-level of activity.

The second report you will find tremendously useful is your Call Activity Report. This report allows you to see who you have called and when, as well as what the outcome was of your calls. If you don't have enough meetings booked on your calendar, this report will tell you why.

Another useful tool you can use is a summary of the requirements, orders, and/or sales opportunities. This report summarizes the activities required to close the sales, as well as the prospective sales pipeline value and the value of the closed sales opportunities. If you want to do some analysis on what percentage of opportunities you have closed in a particular period of time, or analyze how well your sales people are doing, this report will provide that information.

An additional report that is useful is the actual sales report documenting what sales were generated on a monthly basis and how this measures up against your budgeted sales figures for the year. This report can be either very scary or really encouraging depending on how consistent your performance is in bringing in new sales each month.

How to Close Deals

The main lesson each of has to learn when it comes to closing an order is that we should not be afraid to ask for our client's business.

Ask the client what they think the next steps are. In the alternative, you can suggest recommended next steps such as another meeting with other people from your company, a presentation, a proposal, calling your references, or signing a contract.

A "no" is much easier to manage than silence. Remember when you get the client to communicate objections, it is a good sign. You are being given an opportunity to convince the client why she should deal with you and choose your product. If your prospect or client does not give you this information, it will be impossible to sell her anything.

How to Manage Customer Accounts

Once a prospect becomes a client, your work does not stop there. In the same way that you manage a prospect account, you should be all over the client's account. Remember, once you have made one sale, the chances of making additional sales from the same client or someone else in their organization is very high.

At the same time, by serving the customer well and ensuring that you deliver impeccably on all promises, you are creating goodwill and a reference that is like additional money in the bank. Remember your ability to sell is contingent upon how reliable you, your organization, and your product/service are. Once a client has agreed to act as a reference, this increases your chances of closing a future deal with a prospect that had the same need or challenges that your current customer experienced.

Wherever possible, take the time to write a customer testimonial or, better yet, ask him if you can video his testimony and put it on your web site. Remember, documented references are even more powerful than a customer who is willing to give a verbal reference to a prospect. Sometimes your customers may move onto new jobs or retire and not be able to provide a reference any longer. By having a written testimonial, the reference can withstand the test of time and personal and organizational changes.

In conclusion, becoming a master sales person and/or creating a strong sales team is a critical component of every organization. You can have the best product or service, but if you don't have a way of connecting with customers and getting that information to them, the viability of your business will hang by a thread.

I have seen organizations with mediocre products and services but excellent sales and service and have witnessed these organizations rise to amazing financial heights. Sales are an often pooh-poohed competency, without which no company could ever hope to survive or grow. Ensure that you are the best sales person in your field. Ensure that your sales people are at the same level. If they are not, replace them quickly. Do not make the mistake of giving them too much time (more than three to six months) to bring in new sales or you will lose significant momentum that you may never be able to re-coup.

If you look at master entrepreneurs like Bill Gates, Mary Kay, Oprah Winfrey, and Martha Stewart, you will observe that all of them have the strength and unusual ability to sell themselves and their products to the point where their personal identity is equated with the product or service they provide. This is the achievement that we should all seek by finely tuning and honing our personal sales capability and that of our company.

CHAPTER 8
Attracting and Keeping the Best Employees—the "A" Team

Your employees and especially your management team are the life-blood of your business. Choose your team wisely and you will prosper beyond your wildest imagination. Choose your team poorly and you don't have to worry about competition, they will do your business in all by themselves—your very own Trojan horse.

There are cardinal principles in assembling your "A" team. You need to be focused upon two areas—the quality of your people, and the skill sets required to bring your business plan to fruition. When it comes to the quality of your employees, there are several things you need to nail down:

1. The education requirements of the positions you are hiring;
2. The values and personality characteristics required in working for your company;
3. The career and industry experience and the number of years of experience required to fulfill the position;
4. The compensation package, roles and responsibilities, and performance measurements of each position;
5. The processes you will use for recruitment, selection, management of performance, problem/conflict resolution, and termination of employment.

Education Requirements
Determine what education requirements will constitute the minimum you believe is necessary for key positions. Of course, the type of business will determine what kind of education requirements will be appropriate.

Basically, the more education you demand from your employees, the more your business will be able to deliver to your customers. Also, you will be able to use employees in many different capacities, thereby stretching them professionally and improving the productivity of your organization.

If your business is selling products and services to other businesses, versus consumers, university education at the undergraduate and graduate levels will be critical to your growth. In addition, professional designations in your industry might be the minimum many of your competitors hire, to ensure quality and standardization.

Generally, the more sophisticated or complex your business model, the higher the education requirements you will need. Keep in mind that the more educated the people are that work for you, the more versatile and poised for growth your company will be. Basically, any path your business will take will be supported by a strong and extremely capable team.

Values and Personality Characteristics

What kind of company do you want? What kind of culture or work-environment is important to you? These questions are as important to answer as what kind of marriage or family life you want. You will find that the culture of your business is as complex as your most important personal relationships.

Think long and hard about the kind of company you want to work in. Make a list of the non-negotiable values for your company. Let me give you an example.

When I started Knowsys, I decided from the get-go that I wanted to establish a culture that allowed for a strong work and family life balance. As a result, all of the people who work or have worked for our firm have had the opportunity and choice to work from our office, from home, from the client site, or all of the above. I also wanted to create an environment where very intelligent, experienced professionals could learn and feed-off of each other's imagination and knowledge.

Many of the services we provide to customers involve brain-storming, collaboration, and integrating many different points of view to achieve a simple solution to a complex problem.

I also decided early on that no one could work for our company as an "expert" consultant without a minimum of fifteen years experience and having a senior management role in systems integration, Telco, or a financial services company. By senior management, I was looking for people who at the most junior-levels were directors. All these people had a university degree at a minimum, in computer science, engineering, or business.

In addition, we look for certain personality characteristics in all of our employees. Strong work ethics, independent thinking, fearlessness in dealing with difficult situations, strong communication skills, and superlative organizational skills are the most important characteristics we look for.

Another rule or value of our company is that no one is ever forced to do work they don't absolutely love or choose to do. This key value has resulted in our company delivering consulting services that are superlative. Our clients believe that our services are of superior quality and efficacy and, as a result, they are willing to pay a little more for our services.

Clients will often hire us instead of large multi-national firms like IBM, Accenture, or Deloitte to name a few. We are less expensive than these competitors, but clients hire us because we deliver unique knowledge capital or have an impeccable reputation in managing large complex technology and business transformation programs.

Values and personality characteristics of your company's employees translate into revenue and market differentiation, so think carefully about what you want to create.

Career and Industry Experience

Career and industry experience of your employees determine the difference between mediocrity and competence, anonymity, and differentiation in your markets.

Your business model will determine what kind of experience you will hire for your company. I believe that the rule of thumb for what I call complex business models is to over-kill on the skills required to do the critical jobs. This means hiring people who have more experience and talent than is actually required to do the job. This approach has always resulted in exemplary performance and results that have always exceeded the client's expectations.

For simple business models such as retail stores or service providers like doctors and dentist offices, clothing boutiques, hair salons, spas, bakeries, catering companies, etc., the apprentice approach is a productive method of developing good people who are working in entry-level positions. The apprentice approach involves hiring a person with very little experience, but the appropriate educational/professional credentials and having a more senior person teach them the ropes over several years.

The apprenticeship approach is based upon an age-old practice that involves a "master" at a particular profession taking on the development and mentoring of a young person who perhaps has had the professional training or education but no practical experience.

The advantage of this approach is that you can hire someone with great potential at a lower cost and train and mold them in a way that serves your business' best interests over the long-haul. The disadvantage of this approach is that the apprentice may take several months or even years to become fully productive. In light of our culture and the inability of any employer to guarantee life-time employment, employees don't always stick around. Therefore, it can be risky and a poor investment to use the apprenticeship approach if there is a high likelihood of quick turnover in your apprentice employees.

References are a key element of validating an employee's potential in the interview. Better yet, if you have an employee referral program in place, you can have your own employees recommend people they believe are competent and will succeed in your corporate environment. Usually, employers will pay a referral fee after the new employee has passed a particular probationary period.

Compensation Package, Roles, and Responsibilities

They say that good fences make good neighbors. The same can be said for solid employment contracts. An employment contract clearly sets out the terms for employment. It includes the salary, commissions/bonuses, profit-sharing, and benefits. It also includes the performance objectives, timeframes to achieve these, roles and responsibilities, legal obligations and non-competition, and terms for dissolution of employment based on certain conditions that are not met.

At a bare minimum to protect yourself, you should have the following documented and signed by yourself and the employee. If you are hiring a consultant, the same principles apply except that you will frame these documents as a consulting contract, not an employment contract. The minimum documentation you should have in place for all employees, consultants, sub-contractors, or part-time employees are the following:

1. Letter of Offer which sets out the salary, any other compensation, and the benefits associated with employment. Included in the letter of offer should be the terms of probation and the process for termination of employment as well. You may append other documents to the letter of offer that will be relied upon for addressing the parameters for the employee's roles and responsibilities.
2. Roles and Responsibilities Description.
3. Performance Objectives Descriptions.
4. Legal Employment Contract that describes the legal obligations, including non-disclosure, non-competition, protection of intellectual property and company information, including confidentiality of any and all information and knowledge pertaining to employment (excluding any information in the public domain).
5. Benefits booklet.
6. Description of values and ethics and any company strategy/mission information.

Think very hard about the kind of behavior and focus that you want particular employees to have. Do you want an employee to focus on bringing in sales that they drive, or do you want a team-approach to sales? Individual-focused performance requires commissions focused upon individual sales performance. If you want to promote a team approach to maximizing the profitability of a business unit, then you may want to look at providing a profit-sharing program or a team-based performance bonus, based upon sales or profitability.

If your employee is working in the finance or operations department you should consider bonuses based upon cost-reduction results.

Basically, you want to ensure that the employee's focus and behavior is congruent with the compensation rewards you have designed. Not all rewards have to be monetary in nature. You can investigate the use of awards, education, time-off in lieu of over-time pay, sabbaticals, health club memberships, and flex-time/tele-commuting.

If the skills and knowledge of your human resources are in high demand and short supply, your compensation program will need to be extra attractive. You might be vying for the same employees as much larger players and, as such, you will need to be more competitive.

When I started Knowsys Group, the information technology industry was in one of its strongest boom phases. As a result, good people were in very high demand and really short supply. To attract the best and brightest and retain these people, we designed a compensation program and work environment that allowed our people to make significantly more money working for us than our competitors. We also created a work environment that was far more nurturing and flexible with respect to individual employee's needs and interests.

My final comment on compensation is that you should make sure that you document of all of your promises and commitments and always deliver on them. Consult with a corporate lawyer to design an employee or consultant contract that protects your company's intellectual property and confidentiality. It should also ensure that the employee clearly understands their legal and ethical responsibilities to the company and its customers. The other important piece of this contract is termination, and the conditions under which this will be governed.

The last thing you want to deal with is a lawsuit from an un-happy employee who believes that he/she has been unfairly terminated. Having these things spelled out in the contract will minimize potential lawsuits, and maximize a positive outcome if you do have to go down that road.

Human Resources Processes

Regardless of the size and complexity of the business you are running, you will need to address these basic processes inherent in human resource management, at a bare minimum. Documenting these processes could be as simple as noting key points regarding each of these elements on a couple of pages, to writing an actual Human Resources Policy Manual.

My intention is to give you the basic principles that you need to consider to effectively manage your people resources.

Documenting your practices has several benefits, namely, if you forget a promise or commitment or a method of solving an HR problem, you can always refer back to how you intended to solve it by reviewing your documentation. Another reason you should document your processes is that when your company grows, you may have other people handling

Human Resources issues, and as a result, you want to ensure consistency and reliability.

The basic components of a human resources function involve the following processes:

- Recruitment and selection,
- Performance and Compensation Management,
- Problem/Conflict resolution,
- Succession Planning, and
- Termination of Employment.

Recruitment and Selection

For recruitment and selection, you should establish written guidelines and job descriptions to allow for a common understanding of what each position does. If you happen to be advertising or using a recruiter, this documentation can be used to convey the information required to allow both the recruiter and applicant an effective response.

At a bare minimum, you should establish basic questions that all applicants get asked. Where applicable, you might want to have several people in your company interview the prospective employee.

You should also establish your practice with respect to references. Determine what key questions need to get asked and documented. Determine what kinds of references you will need, and how many references constitute a good sample.

A simple, but thorough orientation package and session will also be important when you hire the new employee so that you can properly welcome this new addition to your company and ensure their success by providing them with the information and knowledge required to get up-to-speed quickly.

Performance and Compensation Management

A really important practice to develop is providing regular feedback, praise and reward where appropriate, and constructive criticism when it will help improve the employee's performance. This process can be called performance management.

Performance management should take advantage of informal and formal interventions to create solid communication and feedback to the employees.

Examples of informal interventions are things like impromptu discussions and taking the employee out for a coffee or lunch to discuss how things are going.

Examples of formal interventions are regular weekly, bi-weekly, or monthly performance status meetings with the employee or even a team of employees. Another type of formal intervention is the first "three or six month" probationary review that occurs after the employee starts his job. Usually after that first probationary review, a yearly performance review is done to determine how the employee is progressing, how well he is meeting his performance objectives, and what kinds of additional rewards he can hope to achieve by his outstanding performance.

To be able to carry out a formal performance review, you need to have a well-documented description of the employee's roles and responsibilities. You also need to have a list of all of his performance objectives, and how well he has done against those criteria.

This kind of report card means that you have to establish criteria and related descriptions of what constitutes excellent, very good, good, satisfactory, and poor performance. You should also establish what kind of increases or additional bonuses apply when an employee achieves excellent performance or whatever criteria you feel is sufficient to reward him with a pay increase.

I attended a conference a few years ago on leadership. I had the privilege of listening to Jack Welch, the ex-CEO of General Electric, speak. One of the interesting anecdotes that Mr. Welch discussed was the philosophy that GE followed with respect to performance reviews. He mentioned that those employees who performed at a good or very-good performance level were targeted for retention and development. Those employees who fell into the good-satisfactory were made to understand that their performance fell short of the minimum that GE expected of their employees. Mr. Welch said that these employees tended to leave GE without having to be fired. He believed that those who moved to new jobs because of a mediocre or even satisfactory performance at GE, experienced major epiphanies with respect to overcoming complacent attitudes. He was aware of many ex-GE employees who moved on to new employers and actually became star performers.

Rewards and compensation are closely related or even identical if the only rewards you provide are monetary in nature. If you provide other rewards such as recognition awards and special events, these are not necessarily reflected in the employee's compensation.

Where monetary compensation is concerned, you should document what you will pay each of your employees based upon their position, experience, competence, and seniority. You may want to establish a range of pay for each position. Again the size and complexity of your business will determine how simple or detailed this information needs to be.

Problem/Conflict resolution

In every company there will be the inevitable problems between employees or between employees and their managers. When that happens it is crucial that employees feel that they can make their grievances known and have them dealt with in a fair and respectful manner.

Your problem/conflict resolution process can range from simple and very informal, to complex with many details and variations. Either way you need a few building blocks.

One of these building blocks is communicating your openness in dealing with problems and conflicts and being consistent in listening and communicating resolutions that are fair and respectful to all parties.

Of course you are not always going to be able to solve every problem or conflict to everyone's satisfaction; that may not be possible. But if you can convey respect and sincere interest in dealing with the problem immediately, and a consistent approach to conflict resolution, you are well on your way to creating a viable company culture for managing people fairly.

Succession Planning

If you are planning to operate your business for a reasonably long time, or if you plan to pass it on to a member of your family, or even if you plan to sell it at some time in the future, you need to think of a succession plan.

A succession plan is a conscious decision to groom and prepare bright and loyal employees to take over key positions that are currently occupied, but at a later date might be vacant.

One of the most critical succession plans for you to consider is that one for yourself. At some point, you may not want to work in your business any longer whether out of choice or for health reasons.

If you believe that your business can survive your absence with the right person to replace you, then you need to put a good succession plan in place. Remember, it may take years for you to groom your replacement.

If you decide to sell your business at some point in the future, your ability to demonstrate succession planning for key roles will have a direct impact on the returns of your sale.

If a prospective buyer believes that his/her people can replace you and your key management team members because they see that you already have a team that can cover for each other or even replace one another if necessary, the prospective buyer will be willing to pay more money for the inherent value in your company. This will also lessen the time that you will need to spend with the new buyer after the sale to complete the transition. This scenario increases the chances of taking more of your revenue from the sale of your business up front in lieu of taking most of it at the back end of the transition period.

If you have any inkling that you would like to pass the business on to one of your children or one of their spouses, or some other family member or person of trust, you need to constantly work on your succession plan.

Let me give you a concrete example. An entrepreneur who established a successful dental prosthesis manufacturing company that serves Canada and the U.S. had a dilemma on his hands. How long was he really prepared to work at 150% capacity leading and growing the company? The CEO was already in his fifties and wanted to have more time for other pleasurable pursuits. His choices were to prepare the company for sale or to mentor one of his children to take over the company and continue to grow its revenues.

The child in question was amenable and is now in a multi-year training program, absorbing and learning as much as she can from her father, with the intention of one day being able to play the lead role of CEO of the company. Of course, the founder will always be involved with the company. But with this approach, he will have the latitude and choice with respect to how much time and effort he wants to spend working versus cultivating some of his other interests. From the daughter's point of view, she is jazzed because she knows that she is preparing to take on the role of CEO of this company.

Some of the other aspects that an entrepreneur must consider in his succession plan are what kind of chemistry, communication, and compatibility does he share with the prospective successor. Sometimes these "softer" issues are more important than whether the potential successor has all the skills and knowledge required for the job. In many ways, the new successor will be not only replacing you, but carrying your spirit and vision forward so that your business can thrive and flourish in the future.

For certain key roles like people who lead the way in your sales, customer service/delivery, finance, operations, or marketing organizations, you need to have succession plans in place to address the risk of any key employee leaving. The last thing you would ever want to happen is for you to scramble when a key person leaves and have no one who immediately prepared and trained to step into that position at a moment's notice.

Termination of Employment

Be knowledgeable with respect to the employment laws governing your state or province and what your obligations and limitations are with respect to termination of employment. Under what conditions you terminate employment should be laid out in either the letter of offer or your Human Resources Policy Manual that is provided to the employee upon hiring.

A termination letter should outline all of the critical pieces of information regarding the fact that the employee is being terminated, when the termination will take effect, what compensation is outstanding, and what duties and responsibilities the employee has to his/her employer even after he/she leaves (confidentiality, non-disclosure, etc.). As to the reasons for termination, you should consult your corporate counsel on this issue as what you say can be more damaging to you than what you don't say in writing. Be careful on these issues.

How you terminate employment is a function of your company culture, your industry, and the nature of the termination of the employment.

Generally speaking, if it is possible to have someone else in the room while you terminate an employee then you should do that. There are many advantages to having backup and a witness to the termination. The basic advantages are that you have a witness to all that was said and how the termination was conducted. If there is any litigation at a later date, you will have established a witness to all discussions that pertained to that matter.

In many cases, it is important to have someone else in the room with you from a deterrent perspective. Unfortunately, in my career, I have had to fire a few people. Everyone reacts differently. Some people get very emotionally upset and will break out into tears. Others will get very angry, aggressive, and even in some cases violent. Still others react with strength of character, poise, and grace.

Having a third party in the room with you has a natural, moderating influence on the situation at hand. If the person you are terminating has an angry/aggressive streak, facing two people from the company makes it a lot more difficult for the terminated employee to become aggressive.

Your focus, when you terminate someone, should be on behavior and performance, not on personality issues. Be as compassionate and respectful as possible. Dispassionately review the performance objectives, roles, and responsibilities that have not been fulfilled and reiterate the employment contract's stipulations regarding the conditions for termination.

If you feel that it is feasible to provide the employee with a reference in areas where they were competent or with respect to their character or the length of time and the position they held, by all means do so. But be careful about being either too positive or negative when doing a reference on a terminated employee, because either can cause problems for you of a legal nature.

If the nature of the termination is a layoff or re-structuring of the company, do your best to help the employee secure new employment by providing career counseling, exemplary references, and a reasonable severance pay that reflects what you can afford, but also helps the employee have a reasonable buffer period, so they can reasonably find another job.

Common "Female" Management Pitfalls

No discussion on hiring and keeping the best employees would be complete without discussing our unique "female" management attributes and how they can be a double-edged sword.

I know it is dangerous to generalize, but I have some important insights that I would like to share with you on our unique female nature, based upon having managed and worked with several hundred women in my career both from a corporate and from an entrepreneurial perspective.

Some of our unique attributes that work for us and against us are:

- our natural nurturing/mothering approach in managing and coaching people;
- our ability to manage conflict to create a harmonious environment;
- reverting to a bitchy state when we feel overwhelmed;
- ignoring our intuition to be more rational about all decisions; and
- trying to do all things and to be all things to everybody, but pleasing no one—especially ourselves.

I think we all understand as women how these attributes are positive in nature and how they can help us become great leaders. What many of us don't know, however, is how these attributes can become quite toxic and create a "handicapped" company culture where people don't take ownership of their responsibilities and constantly put their "monkeys" (problems) back on your back to "fix."

Mothering, nurturing, smoothing ruffled feathers are all lovely strengths. But many of us mothers know that, eventually, even a mother has to learn to stop mothering her children—like when they grow up. The same thing goes for a company or corporate environment. You can only mother and nurture employees so much. At some point, when does the mothering stop and when does the employee stand on his/her own two feet, take responsibility for themselves and their results—totally?

Productive, responsible, accountable employees only act this way when you give them the training and tools to do their job and then leave them alone to do it. If someone is not performing, our natural inclination is to help, coach, and even mother them to death, giving them chance after chance after chance, to redeem themselves.

The result is disastrous. Employees perform below par because they believe that the "nurturing" culture of the company means that they can screw-up or screw-around and will still be given a chance to redeem themselves. Better yet, we will step in and save the employee or situation, so that there is no actual negative outcome for anyone.

I have been guilty of this behavior. In trying to create a safe and comfortable environment for my employees, I fostered non-productive employees way beyond the point that I would have expected any employer to have tolerated that performance from me.

As a result, instead of fostering loyalty and superlative performance, I was creating a culture of inconsistent, hit and miss productivity. In a few cases, people actually took advantage of my patience and literally put their feet up and waited to see how long they could do nothing before I would actually fire them.

In the end, my nurturing approach resulted in a lose-lose situation. I lost thousands of dollars of investment in the employee who should have been let go after a few months, or tolerated mediocre performance for much longer than any employer would have afforded me. This resulted in my doing much of the work that my employees should have been doing. The only difference was that I was earning my salary and they were not earning theirs.

So, one of my biggest lessons learned is to be much more decisive and less patient with employees whose productivity is easily measured both from revenue/profitability and industry perspectives. By being less nice and more demanding, I am being kinder to everyone, including myself, the employee, and the bottom line.

A harmonious work environment is what every company strives for. However, if this harmony is achieved by avoiding conflict or by not properly delegating work, then it is a farce. Don't feel that you always have to make every situation all right. Sometimes, conflict, disagreement, and disharmony can be opportunities for learning, growth, even transformation on personal and corporate levels.

Remember, conflict can be a way of productively dealing with problems if each party can be honest about their feelings, believes that they are heard, and the problem has a resolution that is in the best interests of the company. Hopefully, the best interests of the company also are the best interests of the employees. If they are not, the message must be made clear to the employees that the company's best interests will always come first.

Sometimes you will have to be the "bad" guy and make difficult decisions that are not popular. Unfortunately, that is the nature of being a leader. You will need to develop thick skin and learn to live with the concept that you will not necessarily be able to be everyone's friend. Usually, the opposite is true of being a boss, or running a business.

People perceive you as their boss and could never see you as just being their friend. Remember, friends don't have the power to pay you or fire you if you don't perform.

I would also like to address the "bitch" archetype that most of us women struggle with. There is a time and place to be a bitch. Sometimes being nice and polite all the time doesn't work in your interests. People often mistake kindness and courtesy with weakness. As a result, in certain instances being a bitch is necessary with those people who are of this belief. Bitchiness basically allows you to create boundaries with people who don't get the message when it's delivered with sugar.

However, we have to be careful about turning on the inner bitch at inappropriate times and with the wrong people. For example, if we are upset with something that is happening at work, we will often unleash our inner bitch at home, in a very "in your face" way. We may become bitchy with our husbands our children, taking out our frustrations on them instead of the people who are actually the cause of our frustration.

The final aspect of being able to attract and retain the best employees is to work on developing your intuition. We often will have insights that will pop out of nowhere and will be in direct conflict with what our logical or rational minds tell us. How many times does this happen to you? When you listen and act on these insights or intuition, is there a positive outcome?

I have learned the hard way that I must pay close attention to my intuition. In the past, I have worked hard to ignore my intuition, especially when it was in conflict with logic and reason. Through trial and error and many difficulties, I have learned to pay close attention to my intuition.

Being closely aware of how my body feels in certain situations, messages that come into my mind on their own, or as a result of having read something or heard something spoken, or feeling like I have met a person before or I am strongly reminded of another person I know, these are all examples of how my intuition manifests itself.

Sometimes I will get an intuition that something is not quite right with a potential employee during the interview. As a result of this "feeling," I will take extra care in doing references on the person or, in some cases, I will decide that it is not worth taking a chance if I am already feeling misgivings. Of course, I have the benefit of experience I am drawing upon, having interviewed over three thousand people for a variety of professional positions in the computer/information technology industry. So my intuition is backed up by lots of empirical data or experience.

The same thing goes with people who have worked for me. I can tell when an employee is in their groove and is producing great work by his/her results. But more importantly, I can also read my employees' attitudes about their jobs. Are they happy? Do they feel jazzed about their work? Are they determined to get through obstacles? This assessment is done on the basis of facts and my "gut" assessment of the situation. In some cases, the employees have been performing well, but I can see that something is missing in their attitude—a sense of commitment. When I question them about how they are doing, I might find out that they are in the midst of some very real personal crises or that they are not in the position that fulfills them.

My message to you is, listen carefully to your intuition. If you feel that your sense of intuition is not working well for you, you can develop it and improve it, simply by being more aware of how you are feeling in response to external events. You can test yourself on numerous occasions and see if your "gut" is pointing you in the right direction or decision.

Don't ignore your feelings or how your body responds to situations, because you will be missing out on great opportunities for growing your business, attracting the best people, and avoiding major pitfalls.

CHAPTER 9
How to Negotiate Everything

When you think about it, almost everything is a negotiation. From getting your children to complete their homework, to getting your husband to take out the garbage, to negotiating the lease on your work-space, or negotiating a contract between yourself and your customer, every situation poses a unique negotiation scenario.

When it comes to women and negotiation skills I find that we are either of two schools: the push-over academy or the nickel-and-dime university. Either extreme is non-productive and even risky.

I believe the goal of all good negotiators is to strike a deal which is "win-win" in nature. Anything else creates the feeling in one party of being ripped-off. This sets the stage for eventual retaliation of the losing party. The retaliation may occur soon after the negotiations or years after. Regardless of the time frame, it almost always causes more problems and consequences than if the original deal was "win-win" in nature.

What I would like to address in this chapter are the fundamentals of healthy and productive negotiation skills. The framework that I would like to cover will address business negotiations of a simple or complex nature. It can also be used for negotiations of a local and global nature.

The negotiation framework encompasses the following pieces:
1. Pre-negotiation and Preparation
2. Mechanics and Semantics of Negotiation
3. Roles and Responsibilities of Negotiation Participants
4. Supporting Background Information
5. Proposed Agenda
6. Opening Moves
7. Negotiating Tactics
8. The "Deal"

I will go into more detail on what each component of the negotiation process includes and what choices or strategies you can take to achieve your objectives.

Pre-negotiation and Preparation

Pre-negotiation and preparation for the negotiation addresses issues like:

- What are your goals and interests in the negotiation?
- What is your best alternative to this deal? At what point does it make sense to walk away from the deal?
- What are the goals and interests of the other side (your customer, vendor, employee, alliance partner)?
- What is the nature of your/our relationship with the other side?
- Who are competitors for this deal? What is their position likely to be?
- How will the existence of competitors affect your negotiating position?

You must understand the answers to most of these questions to be adequately prepared for the negotiation and to increase your chances for negotiating a deal favorable to you.

Mechanics and Semantics of Negotiation

The mechanics and semantics of negotiation really deals with all of the environmental issues surrounding this activity. For example:

- Where and when should the negotiation take place?
- How long should the negotiation last?
- Have we agreed upon the language, process, and documentation required to complete the negotiation?
- For international negotiations-will an interpreter be required?
- Who will draw up the contract and in what language will it be written?

Although these issues seem to be quite mundane and obvious, you would be surprised how easy it is to assume certain things, or assume that the other side will carry out certain activities without confirming these arrangements. This list is simply a reminder to confirm simple details without which the negotiation could not even occur.

Roles and Responsibilities of Negotiation Participants

A negotiation can be compared to a play or a dance. The only difference is that depending on the nature of the negotiation, the roles and responsibilities of the various participants must be clearly understood and prepared. Otherwise the results of the negotiation could be disastrous-like some kind of orchestrated chaos with no measurable or desirable results.

- Who will the members of our negotiation team be? Who will be our spokesperson?
- Does our team have the right mix of skills and knowledge to complete the negotiation?
- Does everybody clearly understand their role and responsibility on the team?
- Are we adequately prepared as a team? Have we rehearsed our roles and positions during alternative negotiation scenarios?
- What authority does the team have to commit to a position?
- Are there any other third parties that can facilitate this deal?

Whether you are a one-woman show doing the negotiations, or you must rely upon other parties like members of your management team, or your lawyer or your real estate agent, etc., it is extremely important to understand what position or role you and others will play in this dance, and what your desired outcome is likely to be.

Supporting Background Information and Agenda

It is always a good idea to do your research on the party you will be negotiating with. examples of the types of information you should obtain in preparation for this negotiation are articles, biographies, annual reports, and industry reports:

- What kinds of documents do we need to prepare to have the right reference materials in place for the negotiations?

- What consultants or experts will I/we need to hire?
- What documentation do we need to send to the other side in order to adequately prepare them for the negotiations?
- What will our side's agenda be? What will our joint agenda be?
- Does the agenda allow for any surprises or items we would rather not have surface?
- What order will we discuss the agenda items to improve our chances of a successful negotiation outcome?

Opening Moves

Before you actually get into the guts of the negotiations, there are certain items that need to be addressed in the opening discussions:

- Introducing all members of each team;
- Explaining the roles and responsibilities of each member of the team;
- Developing rapport between the team members before getting hot and heavy into the negotiations.
- Introducing and discussing the agenda;
- Agree to the format of the negotiation—who speaks when and how to deal with interruptions;
- Does each party have a clear indication as to what the other party's negotiation authority is?

Negotiating Tactics

Depending on the nature of the negotiations, we will take different tactics to achieve our goals. There are two types of negotiation that comes to mind: the price haggle and trade-off negotiation.

The price haggle is a negotiation that centers on finding middle ground between your number and your opponent's (or the other side's) number. The approach focuses on finding middle-ground between your position and theirs and splitting the difference until you find a position that you both can accept.

The trade-off negotiation is much more complex. It is a negotiation on many different issues and objectives. The desired outcome of each party is that they gain agreement on as many issues as are critical to them while agreeing to concessions on those issues that are not critically important.

Some of the major tactics in any negotiation are:

- Understanding the major issues in the negotiation and their priority to each party;
- Establishing what your strategy will be with respect to each issue;
- Deciding at what point you propose a draft agreement;
- Deciding how you should respond to the other side if it proposes a draft agreement;
- Understand what kinds of non-verbal cues the other side is providing;
- Understanding what options the other side has to obtain to meet its goals;
- Understanding what options you have to obtain your position;
- Deciding what kind of dispute resolution processes should be built into the deal;
- Asking how you are sure that it will be lasting if you do make a deal;
- Understanding what future events and trends might affect the agreement and deciding how to protect yourself against these events;
- Asking if the deal good for both sides;
- Developing a plan for effective implementation of the deal;
- Working out the strategy for managing this deal once the contract is signed;
- Knowing what you need to do to build a good working relationship with the other company.

Remember, when you build and close a deal that is good for both parties, you are building a long-term relationship, not to mention an excellent reputation. If you "screw" the other side and score an excellent deal for yourself and your company, believe me, it will be the last time that you do business with the other party. The other possibility is that you negotiate a great deal that comes back to haunt you; that is, the other side finds every opportunity to exact their pound of flesh on the next deal.

So the moral of this story is to always think win-win. Win-win is the secret to good, long-term deals and developing a reputation for strength, but fairness.

CHAPTER 10
Leadership Lessons from Successful Entrepreneurs

L eadership is an interesting word. It typically conjures up images of generals marching into battle, spiritual leaders evangelizing large groups of people, or heads of state, setting economic direction that affects millions of people.

Leadership in the context of business, and specifically entrepreneurship, is a set of personality characteristics and attitudes that defines success in all of its forms.

If you have ever had the opportunity to read the biographies of successful people—business, political, educational, and arts leaders—you will find many common characteristics these people share.

Many of you reading this book already possess these characteristics. Some of the character traits and attributes that I am going to talk about can be developed through maturity, adversity, and self-awareness.

A leader can be described as a visionary, a coach, a motivator, someone who leads by example, and someone who people will follow to the ends of the earth.

I have met with, read about, and researched some of the greatest leaders in the field of business and entrepreneurship. I would like to describe my thoughts on what constitutes phenomenal leadership and how you can develop these characteristics.

I have listed some of the major characteristics of successful entrepreneurial leaders below. I will describe each characteristic in more detail throughout the chapter. Remember, these are characteristics of "leaders." Only the most successful entrepreneurs will possess all of these attributes. They probably constitute the top 10% of their field.

1. Entrepreneurial leaders feel the fear, but cultivate their courage, and take action anyway.

Vera Wang

It takes a lot of courage to take nothing and turn it into a healthy, profitable company. Vera Wang, one of the top fashion designers today, left a very comfortable position at Ralph Lauren as a Design Director and started her own design house at the age of 40.

Having worked in the industry, Vera Wang understood intimately how difficult it was to operate a profitable design house. Vera was absolutely frightened about starting her own company, but she knew that it was her dream, and she had to get past her worry and fear to achieve success.

She tells an anecdote about how she felt like she was signing her death warrant when she signed the lease for her first store. Her business did not take off right away. She built her business client by client.

Today, Vera Wang is considered a leader in fashion with a global multi-million dollar business. The most beautiful women in the world clamor to wear her creations for weddings, movie premieres, and Oscar Ceremonies. Even with all this success, Ms. Wang is constantly working to overcome fear and anxiety. On a recent Oprah Winfrey appearance she revealed that she takes an anti-anxiety/depressant on a regular basis to manage her constant worry and anxiety. Even phenomenal success does not erase the opportunity for fear and worry.

2. They are passionate visionaries who have the ability to "take charge" in any situation and actualize their dreams.

Mary Kay Ash

"Do you know that within your power lies every step you ever dreamed of stepping and within your power lies every joy you ever dreamed of seeing? Within yourself lies everything you ever dreamed of being. Become everything that God wants you to be. It is within your reach. Dare to grow into your dreams and claim this as your motto: Let it be me." Mary Kay Ash

In 1963, Mary Kay Ash, a single mother, started Mary Kay Cosmetics with just $5,000, her son's help, and a whole lot of faith in herself and her ability to make her dreams real. Today, Mary Kay Cosmetics is a $1 billion company serving 37 markets, with over 350,000 consultants.

Fortune magazine recognized Mary Kay, Inc., with inclusion in

"The 100 best companies to work for in America." The company was also named one of the best 10 companies for women to work for. Her most recent acknowledgements were the "Equal Justice Award" from Legal Services of North Texas in 2001, and "Most Outstanding Woman in Business in the 20th Century" from Lifetime Television in 1999.

It takes so much faith to start something out of nothing and create a company that affects so many people's lives. Mary Kay exemplifies the pioneering entrepreneurial spirit with a vision bigger than most people could ever dream.

When you cultivate your self-confidence, spiritual faith, imagination, and ability to take action you truly can achieve the impossible.

3. They are resilient optimists who turn adversity into opportunity and disappointment and failure into transformation.

Martha Stewart

Entrepreneurial leaders are not afraid of a good fight and will stand-up to anyone or anything that stands in the way of accomplishing their mission.

Martha Stewart is an excellent example of this principle in action. Despite being found guilty of obstruction of justice, serving 5 months in prison, being absent from her business for a considerable period of time, losing significant share value and profitability of her company, and having her reputation and ethics scrutinized and challenged, Ms. Stewart has managed to return with a vengeance for success.

How would you handle such a challenge? Can you imagine the personal and physical toll going to court and fighting for your life would take on you and your family? Can you imagine the humiliation and sense of defeat you would feel after being condemned as "guilty?" What if you sincerely believed in your innocence? What if you were innocent? How would you handle your perception of incredible injustice? Would you become embittered and defeated or would you rise above your ashes like a phoenix and transform your defeat into optimism and continued success?

The company she founded continues to thrive and continues to influence how Americans eat, entertain, and decorate their homes and gardens. In these areas Martha Stewart has influenced Americans more than any one person in American history.

4. Perseverance, nuclear-level energy, hard-work, coupled with excellent sales, communications, and organizational management skills make them un-stoppable.

Estee Lauder

Estee Lauder started her business from inauspicious beginnings, selling her uncle's face creams in a pharmacy. Today, Estee Lauder is a recognized brand name in over 118 countries with $3.6 billion in annual sales and her family's shares are worth $6 billion.

"I have never worked a day in my life without selling. If I believe in something, I sell it, and I sell it hard." This attitude, together with an uncompromising belief in her product and the beauty in all women, made Estee Lauder a respected household name.

How does a woman with no formal education and no special resources or money start a small enterprise that becomes a household name and conglomerate worth billions of dollars? Lots and lots of hard work and the ability to sell her credibility were what defined Estee Lauder's success.

Beyond those pieces of the puzzle, being able to gather the right resources and organize them in a way to continue the business' momentum beyond anyone's wildest dreams, this is the stuff that legends are made of.

5. They have integrity in all aspects of their life and have no qualms about saying "no" to those people and situations that would divert them from their values.

Anita Roddick

A business and a woman, who have become synonymous with alignment of ethics, ideals, and profits, is Anita Roddick of the Body Shop.

Anita gave birth to her business when her husband set off on a trek across the Americas (on horseback) and Anita had to provide for their two daughters. She opened a cosmetic shop in Brighton by the name of The Body Shop. The shop was painted green—"to cover the damp spots," in her words—and had a strong environmental flavor. They had 15 products that she had made herself, which was based on the cleansing rituals of women she had experienced on her travels.

By the time her husband returned from his 10-month trek, she had already opened a second store. She had made a deal with Ian McGlinn for a £4000 loan for half the business. Family and friends ran the first few shops. However, the demand for her shops and products were great, so they set up a franchise system for The Body Shop even though franchising was a relatively new concept in the UK at the time.

From these humble beginnings, The Body Shop grew and then went public in 1984. Today, The Body Shop has over 1980 stores, more than 77 million customers, in 50 different markets and serves customers in over 25 different languages.

When Anita was 10 she had discovered a book about the Holocaust and this had a significant impact on her and influenced her to empathize with the human condition. She has gone on to become one of the most prominent and well-respected social entrepreneurs in the world. These strong social values and conscience are translated into tangible products.

Ms. Roddick frequently donates the profits from particular products to various causes and develops products that highlight a particular region's unique contribution to beauty by leveraging nature and intrinsic artistic talents of that culture. It would have been so easy to abandon this strategy and follow an easier route, focusing on profitability exclusively and social responsibility later—when it was convenient.

In fact, the Body Shop is a great example of how social responsibility created product differentiation and loyal customers from every age and walk of life, all over the world. Anita Roddick proves that integrity does pay if you believe in your ideas and the have the will to actualize them.

6. They have the knack of getting the people, support, and resources required to bring their plan to action. They know how to under-commit and over-deliver.

Ingvar Kamprad

IKEA Founder Ingvar Kamprad made headlines in early 2004 when Swedish business magazine *Veckans Affärer* reported that he had surpassed Bill Gates as the world's wealthiest person. While IKEA's unconventional ownership structure makes this the matter of some debate, there is no doubt that IKEA is still one of the largest, most successful privately held companies in the world, with over 200 stores in 31 countries, employing over 75,000 people and generating over 12 billion in sales annually.

Basically, Kamprad built this multi-billion dollar company from the ground-up. What is really interesting to note is that the growth of IKEA can be attributed to Kamprad's ability to organize and gather resources to enable IKEA's growth trajectory. IKEA's organizational structure is the means by which much of it resources are organized. It is owned ultimately by a Dutch trust controlled by the Kamprad family, with various holding companies handling different aspects of IKEA's operations, such as franchising, manufacturing, and distribution. IKEA even has an investment banking arm.

Kamprad repeatedly resisted pressure to take the company public, feeling that it would slow down decision-making processes and that would slow down growth. It takes a lot of guts and intuition to understand where and how to attract the best resources, people, process, and organizational structure to fuel the growth of your company. Here is an example where going public would have actually been contrary to Kamprad's objectives of growing the company dramatically without interference from outsiders.

An interesting characteristic to note about Kamprad is that he is extremely frugal and yet has made it a habit and a strategy to focus significant corporate resources on charity: On the one hand, Kamprad has a reputation for being, well, "cheap." He takes the subway to work, and when he drives, it's an old Volvo. Rumor is that when he stays in a hotel, if he feels the urge to drink one of those expensive sodas from the wet bar, he replaces it later with one picked up from a nearby convenience store. Yet IKEA has a long tradition of community outreach and philanthropy, with each store encouraged to support local causes, plus international sponsorship of UNICEF and others.

7. They are in tune with their intuition, and as such can spot opportunities that would not be evident to the average person, or assess risk and take prudent action resulting in consistent success.

Debbie Fields—Mrs. Fields Cookies

In 1977, Debbie Fields decided she would open a cookie shop and did just that. In spite of her youth (Debbie was only 20 years old), she won the backing of a banker. She won this backing by leveraging her intuition and making an excellent business case to justify her untried concept.

On August 16, 1977, Mrs. Fields Chocolate Chippery first opened its doors in Palo Alto, California. Halfway through her first day she had not made a single sale, so she went outside and started handing out her cookies for free. Soon people were streaming in to the shop to buy more of her cookies.

Her company motto "Good enough never is", says it all about her business philosophy. The fabulous taste of her cookies, coupled with hard work and customer satisfaction made her business a blossoming success.

Debbie later changed the company name to Mrs. Fields Cookies to allow for other type of cookies than just chocolate chip.

One of Debbie's greatest business innovations was to introduce technology in 1989 for streamlining her company operations. Soon after that, in 1990, she started franchising the business concept. In 1993, she eventually sold out to private investors and turned her attention to motherhood.

8. They are naturally curious and pride themselves on continuous improvement and education.

Marion Donovan—Disposable Diapers

Born in Fort Wayne, Indiana in 1917, Marion Donovan was instilled with an inventive spirit at a young age. She spent the greater part of her childhood hanging around the manufacturing plant run by her father and uncle, two men who combined to invent, among other things, an industrial lathe for grinding automobile gears and gun barrels.

Years later, as a post-World War II housewife and mother of two in Connecticut, Donovan would make good use of the ingenuity that she had observed in her youth. Frustrated by the thankless, repetitive task of changing her youngest child's soiled cloth diapers, bed sheets and clothing, she decided to craft a diaper cover to keep her baby, and the surrounding area, dry. Donovan sat down at her sewing machine with a shower curtain and, after several attempts; she completed a waterproof diaper cover.

Unlike the rubber baby pants that were already on the market, Donovan's design did not cause diaper rash and did not pinch the child's skin. The creative mother subsequently perfected her invention, adding snap fasteners in place of the dangerous safety pins that were commonly used. Donovan named her diaper cover the "Boater" and explained that "at the time I thought that it looked like a boat."

When no manufacturers would even consider her invention, Donovan struck out on her own, and the Boater was an unqualified success from the day it debuted at Saks Fifth Avenue in 1949. Donovan received a patent in 1951 and promptly sold the rights to Keko Corporation.

Her next project was a fully disposable diaper, for which she had to fashion a special type of paper that was not only strong and absorbent, but also conveyed water away from the baby's skin. Donovan took her finished product to every large manufacturer in the country, but once again she found no takers. Incredulously, everyone she talked to told her that the idea was superfluous and impractical. It was not until nearly a decade later, in 1961 that Victor Mills drew upon Donovan's vision to create Pampers®.

In keeping with her inventive heritage, Donovan explored numerous ventures that were completely unrelated to her diaper improvements. She earned a total of 20 patents in her lifetime and also received an Architecture degree from Yale University in 1958.

Although Donovan's extraordinary life may go largely unnoticed by the public, she deserves the undying gratitude of new parents around the globe. It was Donovan's imagination, creativity, and focus on expanding her mind that allowed her to contribute something that would become useful, if not indispensable, to virtually every citizen of a developed country.

9. **They are generous and loyal, giving of their time, insight, knowledge, and resources to enrich others within their company and the community at large.**

Oprah Winfrey

"What material success does is provide you with the ability to concentrate on other things that really matter. And that is being able to make a difference, not only in your own life, but in other people's lives."—Oprah Winfrey.

Oprah Winfrey is probably as well-known for her charitable work as she is for her success in the media world. Some of Oprah's better known charitable works are:

- her Angel Network;
- numerous scholarship funds;
- lobbying for legislative change to protect the interests of children;
- using her show to give people a forum for their creativity and innovation—whether they are selling books or a new product or service; and
- communicating social injustices on her program, while communicating what we can do to change these patterns.

Basically, Oprah's vision for her life is to be an instrument of change, education, and love. Every action she takes reinforces her ultimate goal, which is to better the lives of people who are seeking change and improvement.

In 1989, in a speech to the American Women's Economic Development Corporation, Ms. Winfrey communicated her personal ten commandments:

1. Don't live your life to please others.
2. Don't depend on forces outside of yourself to get ahead.
3. Seek harmony and compassion in your business and personal life.
4. Get rid of backstabbers—surround yourself only with people who will lift you higher.
5. Be nice.
6. Rid yourself of your addictions—whether they are food, alcohol, drugs, or behavior habits.
7. Surround yourself with people who are as smart or smarter than you.
8. If money is your motivation, forget it.
9. Never hand over your power to someone else.

10. Be persistent in pursuing your dreams.

I believe that the fundamental lessons that these entrepreneurs teach us is that you must believe in yourself—your authentic self—not someone you think others want you to be. By believing in yourself, you are sending a message to the world that you and your ideas have value and substance. When you believe in yourself, you become a source of inspiration to everyone around you. People are attracted [magnetized seems a bit odd, but it's your choice.] to someone who exudes confidence and faith.

Difficulties, problems, challenges are a frequent cycle of life that all of us must deal with. Either we learn to master our fears or they master us. Strength is a choice; it is not always an attribute that we are born with. In the same way that a muscle is torn to pieces when you lift a weight, in order for the muscle to grow and become stronger, so does your mind, soul, and will become stronger when you master adversity.

Remember, life is an energy exchange. The more you give of yourself to others, the more you develop and continually reinvent yourself, the more life gives back to you. Change and transformation are constant companions for the successful entrepreneur.

PART 3
Reaping the Benefits Cycle

CHAPTER 11
Understanding How to Manage for Financial Stability and Growth

There are so many ways that you can slice and dice financial stability and growth. If you look at it from the perspective of running your corporation, financial stability and growth means good cash-flow, healthy cash position, high profitability, and year-over-year revenue growth.

If you answer the same question from a personal perspective, the answer is healthy savings, healthy investments, no debt, and money to spend on things that are important to you and your family.

Your business is a means to an end. That end can take many perspectives.

Your business can allow you to:

- Be independently wealthy
- Create your retirement income
- Live a fulfilling life

It can also:

- Be what you do until the day you die (hopefully out of choice not necessity);
- Create enormous income that you squander on non-value items;
- Create heavy debt from living beyond your means;
- Create a feast or famine spending and living pattern;
- Create a fast-paced, but burdensome life.

Your business is a double-edged sword. It can cut for you or against you, based on how well you manage your finances. How well you manage your business affects the income you have available to create personal wealth. These are very different skills. For example, a CEO could manage her company finances quite successfully, creating immense income for the corporation and for herself, personally. At the same time, she could be a total disaster on the personal front. She could spend more than she makes, racking up crippling debt.

Entrepreneurs are notorious for being high rollers when it comes to making money, spending money, and borrowing money. They are not always as well known for frugality or prudence with their finances.

Women entrepreneurs do break this general pattern. They tend to be much more conservative than their male counterparts. Being conservative with your finances is an excellent characteristic to build upon. Marrying conservative financial management with shrewd analysis of how to create sources of income and measured risk-taking is a recipe for financial independence.

In this chapter, we will examine the best practices for healthy financial management of your business and your life. Both are intertwined. If you do both well, you will be unstoppable.

Financial Management Best Practices for Your Corporation

At your lowest level of capability as a CEO, your job is to ensure that your company generates an income from which you can fund the salaries of yourself and all of those who work for you, as well as your overhead expenses.

The second level of capability is that you generate additional income that funds the growth of your company, allowing you the opportunity for investments in additional human resources or other capital like knowledge, real estate, and infrastructure.

The third level of capability is that you attract further investment in your company, either privately or in the form of going public. As a result of this infusion in capital, you expand your business on a global basis or dramatically expand your product and/or service portfolio.

The fourth level of capability is that you seed other companies that generate income as separate entities. These separate companies could be related companies in that they share the same name, but have different divisions. They could also be completely different lines of business, completely unrelated, allowing for diversification of your capital. At this level, your company also invests heavily in charities and giving back to the community .

The fifth level of capability is a company that is so immensely profitable and independent of the persona of the founder that it becomes attractive to a much large corporation, interested in acquiring smaller companies.

1st Level—Cover Your Salaries and Overhead

Most small or start-up businesses never make it past this level. Covering your expenses—your salary, the salaries of your staff, and any other overhead expenses is a critical requirement, if you are going to stay in business.

If your goal is to have a business that pays you a modest salary and gives back to the community in the form of employment of people, the first level of financial maturity is ok. If you want your business to flourish and grow, you will have to move past this point and learn how to generate additional income.

An interesting facet of not creating income in a privately-owned business is the concept of creating so many expenses that benefit the owners that the net income left over is negative or null. This result creates a situation where your company pays little or no tax. Many privately owned companies look to achieve this situation.

When you minimize your corporate taxable income, the behind-the-covers story is what you are making after you sell your products or services. If this is a significant gross profit, your business is essentially profitable. How you decide to spend that profit is up to you of course. If you want to get access to lines of credit, it is wise to show a few years of net profit, in addition to gross profit.

Your accounting firm can provide you with excellent strategies to minimize the corporate income tax you pay. They can also help you structure your company in such a way that you will minimize corporate income taxes paid out if you sell your company at some time in the future.

Legitimately minimizing the corporate tax you pay is a significant component of your financial strategy. By minimizing your taxes, you essentially have more access to your company's revenue to pay salaries or other fixed expenses necessary to fuel your company's growth.

To be able to pay salaries and other overhead, tight cash management is another element of your financial management strategy. Each month, either you or your accountant/controller should prepare a cash position report. The cash position report contains the following critical elements:

- Balances of all of your corporate bank accounts at a particular point in time. I like to have a snapshot at the beginning of each month.
- A listing of all of your outstanding accounts receivable.
- A listing of all of your outstanding payroll commitments.
- A calculation of the revenue generated in the previous month.
- A summary total of all salary expenses.
- A gross profit calculation (revenue-direct expenses such as salaries) for the previous month.

This cash position report allows you to understand how much working capital you have left to work with after you pay your salary commitments. If your cash position is growing each month, that is, your working capital is growing, then you have tangible evidence of your company's financial growth. If the opposite is true, you will have a detailed view of what salary expenses you are paying out and if it is time to consider letting people go in order to improve your gross profit position and ultimately the cash you will have on hand.

Many entrepreneurial businesses fail to manage their cash and, as a result, get a terrifying surprise when they unexpectedly do not have the cash available to pay salaries or other non-discretionary expenses.

Another important habit to develop is to avoid incurring debt. My policy has been and will continue to be, "no debt." That means that aside from our line of credit, which is paid down as soon as our accounts receivable comes in, we retain no debt. Business expenses incurred on credit cards are paid down fully each month for each employee. All bills for products, services, supplies, are paid down fully each month.

If I notice that our cash position has been decreasing, I will tell everyone in the company to stop spending money, except on those things that will generate revenue.

The opposite is true as well. If I see that our cash position has been steadily growing and we have reached a particular milestone, I will put away some of that capital to make an investment in hiring a new employee or upgrading our technology infrastructure or even open a new office in another location.

In addition to the cash position, an income statement for each month that documents your company's cumulative financial performance from the beginning of the fiscal year until that point in time is another tool you will use often. The monthly income statement allows you to understand the patterns in growth or contraction in your revenue and all expenses to date. When I would analyze the income statement and see that we were making significant net profit on a monthly and cumulative basis, I would panic.

I would panic because if we continued to make such a significant amount of money without continually investing in important facets of our company, like bringing on new employees, or expanding our premises, or investing in new marketing materials and advertising, we would end up paying a lot of money in income tax, instead of investing that money in areas that would help our company to generate more income in the long run. I specifically remember our early years when I didn't have that knowledge. I would learn at the last minute that it was a few weeks before the end of the fiscal year, that our company had made significant net income.

My choices were to pay that money to the government or invest some of that money in expenses that would prepare our business for the next level of growth. I remember last-minute shopping runs to Business Depot to stock up on supplies, computers, software, chairs, desks, whatever our company happened to need, but I had been too frugal to buy during the year, for fear of using up our cash on discretionary, but non-essential items.

The reason everything was done at the last minute is that in the early days, my part-time accountant could not enter all of our expenses in a timely manner into our general ledger. As a result, we would only have the expenses compiled and entered at the end of the year, and that was when we knew that we were in pleasant trouble. It was time to shop or invest in things we had held off on all year.

After doing this for a few years and being profitable every year, with the exception of one year, I invested in additional accounting staff, better accounting software. Today our general ledger is up-to-date and I get monthly income statements. As a result, we do very little last-minute spending anymore.

Another useful tool is that of a monthly sales report. The sales report should contain the budgeted sales for each month on an aggregate and on an individual, departmental, or regional basis. The actual sales performance for each month and the cumulative total should be compared to the budgeted monthly and cumulative figures in this report.

The value of the sales report is that it allows you to see how your team is performing from a sales perspective. If a sales person or sales team is consistently missing their targets, you have the information you need to intervene and hopefully get them back on track. If it looks like your sales figures are trending much lower than your forecasts, then it is time to rein in your expenses to compensate for the decrease in your revenue performance.

The final element of the first level of financial maturity is to establish a budget for all major expenses. Each month you can track your actual expenses against your budget to determine how closely you have managed the expense element of your operation.

The most important message I can give for those of you who are operating at this level is that you have to pay close attention to your financial details each month, with a hard focus on your cash position and consistently growing your company's working capital.

Do not spend money you don't have or run up credit card debt, especially when your revenue streams are inconsistent or decreasing over time. Even if your revenues are increasing over time, make it a habit to pay down your credit cards each month.

2nd Level—Funding Growth

The second-level of financial maturity is that of funding the organic growth of your company. By organic growth, I mean growing your company from the profits you generate, as opposed to borrowing money from the bank or seeking outside investors.

If you are closely managing your cash and intimately understand your monthly and cumulative net income and if you are on top of your game with respect to revenue, you have all of the bases covered.

At this point it is time to kick your financial competence up a level, by working on your growth game.

There are several ways to grow your business:
- grow your revenue
- expand your operations geographically
- expand your customer base
- invest in income producing-ventures

Growing revenue can be achieved in many ways. You can hire more experienced sales people to add to your management team. You can also invest money in additional marketing, such as public relations, press releases, seminars and conferences, trade show participation, web site/e-commerce and brochures.

If you are in a manufacturing facility, you can also expand your operations by adding staff and/or capital, purchasing new real estate, or leasing new facilities.

I have a word of warning for you. If you expand your business, make sure that you put aside the money you require for this expansion, even if you borrow money from the bank to do so.

For example, if you borrow money from the bank to buy equipment and tools for a manufacturing or renovation business, ensure that you put aside the additional revenue/profit you are making to service your debt. Design a plan to pay down your debt very quickly, let's say within 1-3 years.

Don't make the mistake of spending the additional money you are making on nonsensical spending luxuries, including cars, boats, clothes, etc. if you are taking on debt to finance the growth of your company. Plan for the worst and be conservative with your money. Remember, most new businesses go bankrupt within a few years of start up. They often go bankrupt because owners get into the habit of expecting that the business will grow continuously and indefinitely and consequently spend their newly found profits on personal luxuries, thinking that they will always have the profits to fund their line of credit. The problem occurs when the profits stop growing and the business starts to level off or even to contract.

Every business is subject to cycles, ups and downs. Most entrepreneurs make the mistake of overextending themselves because they think the money train will just keep running through. So enjoy your growth, but be careful. It is an opportunity to create unbelievable abundance for your company in the long run, but it is also a potential pot hole if you don't plan for sustained growth.

3rd Level—Outside Investments

The third level of financial maturity is creating a company with the profitability and characteristics of an organization that can generate higher than average returns for investors.

At this stage, you have the choice to consider and invite outside investors or lenders to provide you with the money required to grow your business to the next level.

If you look at the history of large, global companies that started off as entrepreneurial organizations like Ford, Microsoft, Oracle, Ikea, Amazon, and Google, at some point it is unavoidable to go outside of your working capital to expand your business. You may have to do this if you want to realize the potential growth that you have identified.

Earlier in the book, I discussed the alternatives with respect to outside funding. So you are well aware of the pros and cons of borrowing large sums of money from the bank, or trading your control in your company for funding from venture capitalists.

Another choice for entrepreneurial company's looking to grow exponentially is going public. Basically, you put up a piece of your company for sale to the public in the form of shares.

There are many advantages to going public. Some of these advantages include lots of money to fund your growth, global visibility, instant credibility, and prestige. Some of the disadvantages include the expense required to go public, scrutiny of the public and regulators, accountability to thousands of people beyond your employees, and short-term financial performance focus.

Going public is not cheap. You will need a law firm that specializes in IPO's. You will also need an accounting firm that can help you restructure your financial management processes, especially with respect to financial reporting requirements. You will need to hire a public relations firm or hire a team that will focus only on public relations and communications. At any rate, after all is said and done, your company will have incurred millions of dollars in fees just to go public.

Besides your "one-time" fees to go public, you will have to hire additional people to conduct your accounting, financial reporting to regulators, communications, and public relations. Your internal financial reporting will have to be significantly more stringent than that of a private company.

You will also have to make financial and organizational provisions for implementing Sarbanes Oxley regulations. This in itself can constitute millions of dollars of additional cost on a one-time and a perpetual basis. Sarbanes Oxley is the legislation that the U.S. government has put into place to ensure that financial and operational controls are in place to minimize the opportunities to mismanage funds and information, resulting in financially misleading results to shareholders. This legislation is designed to minimize the abuses of companies like Enron, Adelphia, and Worldcom.

You should have your finance people do a thorough business and financial analysis of what it will take to go public. Think long and hard about what price you are willing to pay for growth. If you clearly understand the pros and cons, the costs and the benefits and you still believe this is viable, go for it.

4th Level—Seed New Companies

The next level of financial maturity is having the financial resources and brain power to seed new companies. This approach of seeding new companies allows you the opportunity to diversify your financial risk; expanding the wealth and contributions you are making to your community and economy and has the potential to create an exit strategy for you should you decide to sell your original company at some time in the future.

Seeding a new company could involve starting a wholly-owned corporation where you are the majority shareholder. It could also involve your investment in another company with the majority shareholder being someone other than you. This approach can be useful when you are trying to create some distance between you and other members in your family that were working in your company originally. You may have your father or son run this new company, but you are a lesser shareholder.

There are numerous financial and tax benefits of starting another company. If you are not the majority shareholder but a major investor, you may be able to take advantage of additional income generated for you but be taxed at a minimal amount. From a legal liability perspective, splitting your financial resources into separate companies can provide significant protection from potential law suits and protection from creditors. This is something that has to be planned and implemented with the help of your accountants and corporate tax lawyers. Additionally, from a capital gains perspective there could be significant tax breaks for you as well.

Your job as CEO is to continually create ancillary streams of income from as many sources as you can. Investing in other companies, where you have a strong sense of the company's potential or where you can input your knowledge and talent, is an excellent way to create new income.

On another level completely, investing in new ventures creates more wealth and abundance in the community at large. If you are in a position to invest in new companies, you should also seriously consider how you can contribute to your community through charitable donations. There aren't any rules regarding how much you should be donating. However, the spiritual rule of thumb is 10% (tithe) of your income. How much you give to charitable organizations is a choice you make based upon your heart and your love of fellow humanity. Giving does create an immense high and is part of a spiritual cycle that renews you—the giver—with a sense of how connected we all are in the grand scheme of things.

When your company has the capacity to give back to the community, you have reached the pinnacle of financial success. Not only are you able to enrich the lives of those who work for your company, but you are also able to enrich the lives of many other people, who will hopefully do the same for their fellow citizens. You have created a tremendous cycle of abundance and good will for everyone your company touches.

5th Level—Sell Your Company

At this level of financial maturity, you have made a lot of money for yourself and everyone that your company has touched. At some point, you may decide that it makes sense to sell your business and go off and do something new.

If your company is still privately owned, you can approach organizations that specialize in match-making between buyers and sellers. The next chapter provides the details of how to sell your business.

If your company is publicly owned, you have the option to sell all your shares or just a portion of them. If you want to extricate yourself from your company to retire or go on to other things, you will have to work with the board to determine a succession plan, basically identifying who will replace you.

As an owner of a company that you have worked hard to build and grow over many years, you will want to sell your company, so that you make enough money to cover the company's value, but also to cover several years of future income for yourself. How you come up with the value of your company is rather complicated. Chapter 13 covers how you evaluate the value of your company.

Personal Financial Management Best Practices

Remember my earlier point about how notorious entrepreneurs are for feast and famine financial behavior. Entrepreneurs generally are great spenders, but not very good savers or investors.

What is your financial behavioral blueprint? Let me give you a couple of guesses. Look back at your first family—your mom, dad, siblings. How did your parents handle money? What kinds of values did they hold about money? Was money considered to be a necessary evil? Was it saved, but rarely spent, because they thought that it would run out? Did your parents cycle between big spending and then telling you that they were "broke?" Were you comfortable—neither poor but not necessarily well off? How do your parents live today? Do they have a healthy retirement income, or do they live pension cheque to pension cheque?

Your financial management quotient (fmq) is a function of everything you were taught about money from your parents multiplied by your earning power to the power of your self esteem.

The equation looks like this:

personal wealth = parent's values x your earning power x your self esteem

Personal wealth is more about your values and beliefs about money and your self esteem. You can make millions, but if you don't feel happy within yourself or if you believe that money is basically evil, you will find every possible opportunity to sabotage your success. If you feel that your wealth is more about what you show to the outside world—your possessions, as opposed to the joy that you experience in living—you may create ill financial health.

There are several habits that you need to develop to become financially healthy and wealthy:

1. Learn to live below your means.

No matter how much money you make, you should always make it your habit to live below your means. What do I mean by this? I mean, spend significantly less than you make. Why? Spend less than you make for peace of mind. This will allow you to have the ability to sleep at night, because you don't owe money to anyone, and because you can still make ends meet, even if your personal income decreases for some unforeseen reason.

Having your own business means that anything can happen, anytime. What goes up can come back down. So, don't make the mistake of spending like the money train will never stop running. I am not saying not to spend on things that are important to you to enjoy your life. Just spend so that you have lots of income left over for unforeseen circumstances.

2. Prioritize your spending to maximize your joy.

If you want to be truly wealthy and successful, you must understand yourself inside, out, and backwards. What makes you happy? What makes you anxious? What do you feel that you owe your family? Do you love your life?

When you understand what makes you and your family happy, you will establish what your priorities are with respect to spending.

Is it a priority to have a lovely home for you and your family? Is it a priority for you to travel regularly? What about private schools for your children? Are they your priority? Are cars, designer clothes, and jewelry important to you?

Understand what constitute priorities for you, your husband, and your family's needs and focus your spending on these items. It is easy to spend money on useless, no-value things that bring no joy, but quickly chew-up your disposable income.

3. Eliminate or minimize your personal debt.

The most powerful benefit that owning your own business can deliver is an income stream that allows you to do away with personal debt. As you pay down personal loans, lines of credit, and credit cards, your sense of personal freedom and empowerment will grow. This was the first thing I did as soon as I started to make money from my business. Before I went out and did any big, fun spending, I systematically paid down all the debts.

It is also important to establish a habit of paying down your personal debt every month. For example, pay down your credit cards completely each month and, if possible, buy as much as you can with cash.

Getting into the habit of using cash for your daily living expenses is an excellent habit to get into, especially if you have a history of getting out of hand with credit card spending.

4. Systematically save a portion of everything you make (at least 10%).

Every time you deposit a pay cheque in your account, make it a habit to take at least 10% of your cheque and put it into a savings account. When you hit certain milestone amounts in your savings account—for example, every time you hit $10,000—you can instruct your bank to transfer the money to an investment account (treasury bills, bonds, GIC's, or mutual funds).

Make sure that whatever investment you choose to put this money into is secure, so you don't lose your principal. Of course, your rate of return won't be as great, but remember, this is your savings, and you will want to have preserved the principal and added some additional interest to it to use for paying down your mortgage, or buying another piece of real estate, or simply having a contingency fund (Oh Shit Fund) for unforeseen emergencies.

5. Pay off your mortgage on your primary residence as soon as possible.

Once you have established a habit of paying down your credit card debt and any other personal loans, you are ready to start paying down your mortgage. You can establish a habit of paying down additional sums on your mortgage like doubling your monthly payment or paying down the maximum allowable amount on the anniversary of your mortgage.

If you have a short-term mortgage or even a mortgage of an open nature, you can pay down your whole mortgage in just a few years. Don't get distracted by the large income you are making and getting sucked into nonsensical spending. You would be surprised how quickly you can "piss" away several thousands of dollars each month that could otherwise be used to pay-off your mortgage.

6. Become a tax expert to legitimately minimize the personal tax that you make.

Another very intelligent way to maximize your income is to educate yourself on the tax laws that pertain to individuals and corporations. Make sure that you maximize your deductions, that you keep copies of all of your receipts, and that you get an accountant's help to complete your tax return accurately and correctly.

By maximizing your tax deductions, you will maximize the income that you earn. Again, plan to save some of the money you get back from the government or to apply it against your mortgage. Make sure that you retain all files and copies of receipts associated with your returns for at least seven years.

7. Create additional streams of income from your savings.

After having paid off all of your debts and mortgage, you are ready to create additional streams of income outside of your business. You can do this in a number of different ways. You can invest in:

- Bonds
- Stocks
- Guaranteed Investments
- Mutual Funds
- Commodities
- Real Estate

If you are going to invest in stocks, bonds, and mutual funds, make sure you are well-educated on your investments and the companies they encompass. If investments are not your forte, find a reputable and knowledgeable investment advisor to help you manage your risk and make money according to your objectives.

You should make it a habit to read at least one financial management book or at the very least several articles a month, to keep yourself educated and aware of what opportunities for investment there are out there.

If you are like me and spend a lot of time in the car, buy audio tapes or CD's by various financial management gurus like Suzie Orman and David Bach, and play them while you are driving to meetings.

When it comes to investments, I have a bias towards real estate. I have never lost money, but have made generous profits on real estate. I love that I can take advantage of tax write-offs with respect to my real estate investments. The proviso to this recommendation is that you should be able to easily carry the mortgage on a real estate investment, even if you cannot rent out the property for several months.

If you are tight with your income and would be in serious trouble if you could not rent your property for six months or more, don't buy it. I have met so many people who have stretched themselves so thinly, that when push came to shove, they had to sell their property at fire sale prices, losing money and owing the bank money, because the mortgage was more than the selling price.

When you think of income-generating investments, real estate is an excellent consideration because it generates income, tax deductions, and capital gains down the road when you sell it. The advantage of investing in real estate is that you leverage debt (other people's money, i.e., banks) to create income for your family.

What is a reasonable level of investment with respect to your income? If you are on the conservative side of things, 10% of your income is a reasonable standard with respect to investing. If you are more on the aggressive side of things, 30% would be a fair representation of an aggressive investor. It all depends upon your income and your ability to eliminate consumer debt. If you have successfully done this and paid off your mortgage, you could potentially be left with a lot of money in savings which you should invest.

If you do invest 30% of your income, divvy it up and spread your risk. Put most of it in safe investments (60-70% of this investment pool)—with guaranteed rates of return. Put no more than 30% of this amount into riskier investments—stocks, commodities, and real estate.

My main point here is to invest your money wisely and look for ways to create other streams of income outside of your business. It is so easy to be tempted into squandering your money on nothing. I know because I have done that and learned the hard way that those hundreds of thousands of dollars spent on luxuries don't create any lasting value. I am not saying that you shouldn't spend money on luxuries—just make sure that you are investing at least as much money as you are spending on frivolities.

8. Maximize your retirement savings.

In a way, I really don't see retirement savings as an investment or a discretionary item. To me it is a dire necessity to focus on and plan for, and most importantly to execute upon.

If you have your own business, no one is going to offer you a pension, except for you. That means that you have to understand what your income needs will be when you stop working, wind down or sell your business. Here I suggest that you work very closely with an investment advisor who comes well-recommended.

I have to say that I have had several investment advisors since I started working. Some were ok. Some were just plain awful. Recently, I got smart and started asking financially savvy people who managed their portfolios. I got a recommendation to an investment advisor who understands the importance of an integrated investment and retirement savings plan.

My investment advisor is Stan Teppner, of CIBC. His approach is to work very closely with my accounting firm, our law firm, and our insurance guy, to create a money-making strategy that leverages all of my corporate advantages and works in concert with all of the people who understand my financial and corporate situation intimately.

I would say that this approach is extremely unique. Until now, I have seen no evidence of this approach in other banks and brokerage houses that I have dealt with in the past.

So, if you think carefully about what your business will fetch after you sell it, what your real estate and equity investments are generating, along with your savings, and forecasted expenses (at age 65 or 70), then you get the picture of what you need to be saving in order to create a comfortable income.

Pay attention to this now, while you are young and making money and have the health to make things happen. For those of you starting a business at a later age, hopefully you have a pension from your previous employment or you have already started investing in your retirement savings from an early age.

I am sure that after you start to do some of the calculations, you will understand the importance of being careful with your spending, because you could be literally pissing away your future. Take heed!

9. Establish an "oh shit!" fund equal to one year's salary.

What is an "oh shit!" fund? Very simple; it is the money you would need to live on in the case of some kind of personal calamity or disaster.

Why save one year's salary you ask? I say why not? We live in such capricious times. As businesses can boom beyond expectations, so can they bust. If your business busted for some reason, you would need a source of income to live while you revived, transformed, or looked for a job, wouldn't you?

I have worked in the information technology industry since 1982. Over the last twenty-four years, I have witnessed phenomenal change in my industry. Where prospective employees were interviewing and screening potential employers in the late 1980's through the late 1990's, today I know several sharp, super-experienced senior technology people who have been out of work for six months or more.

The information technology industry was supposed to be an industry where demand would always outstrip supply, but today this is not the case, probably in large part due to outsourcing. Therefore, there are lots of competent, skilled people out there looking for work who can't find it. If you were in this position, wouldn't you sleep better at night knowing that you had a year's grace to find the proper job or business for you, as opposed to being desperate and just taking anything to pay the bills?

The other element that is unique for us women is that we may get unexpectedly pregnant. Although many of us have worked right up to the moment of labor (I know I did), you may need to take time off during the pregnancy due to premature labor (I was on my back for 4 weeks with both my boys). If this happens to you, how will you pay the bills? Perhaps you will need to hire someone to replace you for a few months.

The other possibility is that your child needs your care, due to illness (God forbid!). This happens to many people, and always at a time when you least expect it.

Another very real crisis that can occur is divorce. If you are in this position, sometimes it can be very difficult to concentrate on your business when your life is falling apart. Having that "oh shit!" fund gives you some room to breathe. If you have to take some time off work, or if you must pay expensive legal bills, your contingency fund will be invaluable to you.

The irony of a contingency plan is that if you have one in place, you probably will never need to take advantage of it. Unfortunately, due to good old Murphy's Law, the opposite is true. If you fail to plan, you plan to fail. Don't put yourself in a vulnerable position by avoiding these realities. Put aside at least one year's salary for you and the same for your husband.

10. Leverage your credit rating by maximizing the personal line of credit available to you.

Let's assume for a moment that your business has done fabulously well and you have established a multi-million dollar net worth for yourself. Take advantage of your stellar financial position and credit worthiness and get as much leverage as you can from your banker in the form of high credit card limits and a substantial line of credit.

You may be quite perplexed at this point at my advice. Didn't I just admonish you to save, save, save, and pay-off all debt? Now I am encouraging you to go out and maximize your debt. What gives??

What gives is the following. Wealthy people have access to very low rates of interest (at or below the prime rate). If you are a wealthy person, it is prudent to maximize these advantages. No one says you have to use them or abuse them. But think of the peace of mind as well as the necessity of having significant lines of credit at times when your cash flow is slow. This can happen to even the best business if, for example, their customers are very slow to pay.

If you are diligent about using a fraction of your allowable credit and paying it down diligently, you will establish a superlative credit rating. This will go a long way toward getting additional loans for your business down the road. Remember, to the banker, if you are the major or sole shareholder of your company, your credit worthiness reflects well, or not on your business' credit worthiness.

11. Ensure that you have sufficient disability, critical care, and life insurance to more than cover your income.

In addition to the other contingency measures I spoke about earlier, insurance is a very real necessity if you are self-employed. Remember if you get injured or sick, no one will pay you a salary, except your company if you have sufficient working capital to do so. But even if you have the resources in your company, you should seriously pursue disability insurance. At the very least you should buy it for yourself, and if you can afford to provide it for your employees, it is a worthy investment.

In addition to disability insurance, you should look into critical care insurance. This is a little different than disability insurance in that you are given either a lump sum if you get one of the listed diseases (breast cancer for example) or the insurance company will pay for you to receive the absolutely best treatment, even if that means having to travel to another country. Considering the prevalence of cancer, heart disease, and diabetes in our society, and how disruptive being sick can be on you, your family, and your business, critical care insurance is an excellent idea.

It is very difficult to imagine our own death, but unfortunately, it is a road we must all travel at some point in time. If it happens to be earlier rather than later and your children still require emotional and financial support, life insurance is another necessity you should not ignore.

You should purchase enough life insurance to allow your husband and children to live off the premium for as many years as the children would have required your support. For example, if you are earning $200,000 per year and your children are 10 years old when you die, you will need an amount equal to your income for at least 12 years (until your kids have completed university). The amount in this case would be $2.4 million. Sit down and speak with an experienced life insurance person— hopefully someone who can work closely with your investment advisor, accountants, and law firm, to establish what your bare bones needs are.

Another consideration with your life insurance is having a sufficient pay-out so that your husband could hire someone else to replace you to continue running the business. This sum of money might be in addition to the earlier sum mentioned. So as you can see, this is not a subject to be sloughed off to my "I'll do it later" list.

12. For God's sake, make sure you have a properly executed will.

All this planning and great investment strategies will mean absolutely nothing if you don't have a properly executed will and a living will prepared by your lawyer. Remember, your case is probably not your run of the mill will because you own a corporation. Most likely, a significant portion of your money will stay in your business in the form of working capital. How does your husband or executor get access to that money when it belongs to the corporation and only you can make withdrawals on your corporate accounts? If you are dead, how will money be taken out of the company?

All of these things must be considered and factored into your will.

Also, remember the case of Terry Schiavo, the brain-dead woman who was the subject of legal battles between her husband and parents. One side wanted to continue keeping her alive (her parents); her husband wanted to pull the plug. A living will would have solved the problem. But, if you don't have one, you are setting yourself and your family up for infinite heartache.

Be smart. Attack this task like your life and that of your family depends upon it, because—guess what—it does!

Money is an emotionally-charged subject, even for a business. You should really dig down deep and understand what money means to you and your family. Be cognizant of behaviors that sabotage or support the flow of abundance to you.

As women, one of our behavior patterns, even if we make a lot of money is to hand-off our earnings to our spouses and trust that they will manage it for us. If this has been your behavior pattern, stop it right now. This habit is unhealthy for both you and your spouse. You should pay attention to where all of your money is, how it is invested, what you owe in terms of bills and debts. You should also hammer out a plan with your spouse that addresses your finances for the short—and long-term. Basically, take the same due diligence you apply to your business and exercise it heavily in your personal finances.

Remember you have the power to make millions, even billions. You also have the power to squander millions. Pay attention to your thoughts, emotions, attitudes, and instincts when it comes to money. It really isn't how much money you have, but how you live that determines your happiness quotient. Know yourself well, and let money express your values and deepest needs. This practice will serve you well and will always create a flow of generous abundance from the universe.

CHAPTER 12
Managing Family Politics without Strangling Anyone

T he reality that most entrepreneurs must deal with is that they are leading and managing businesses where their husbands and other family members are integral parts of the management team.

In many instances a woman has started a company, and once it has become a going concern, other members of her family, like her husband for example may join her to provide the support, motivation, and know-how to grow the business to the next level.

The business may become a large enough going concern so that your brothers, sisters, parents, even in-laws may become involved in running different parts of the business.

Unfortunately, the need for incorporating family into your business usually becomes a blessing and a curse. Family can be a blessing from the perspective of loyalty, hard work, and a feeling of ownership in the results and growth of the company.

Family can become a curse because of the same reasons that they are a blessing. But add family politics to that mixture and an inability to behave professionally, because they cannot step out of family-mode communication into the realm of business practices and work place rules of engagement, and you have a recipe for daily warfare and a toxic work environment.

Let me illustrate with a few anecdotes.

One of the examples I have come across in my travels is that of a family-owned business that had been in existence for many years. Basically, the brothers had built a construction business from the ground up and had equal ownership. The business had gone through good and bad cycles but had thrived for several decades. Then an inevitable thing happened. One of the brothers died and his children, who had already been involved with the business for several years, took over his ownership of the company when he died.

While their father was still alive, he buffered his children from all of the family politics he dealt with on a regular basis.

At about the same time that their father died, one of their uncles decided to retire and to give his share of the business to his children. As a result, the new management team and board of the company were made up of some of the original owners who were brothers and the new owners who were nieces and nephews of their uncles.

The sister and brother, who were much better educated than their uncles and even some of their cousins, were given additional executive management and sales responsibilities for the company.

During regular board and management meetings of the company, the atmosphere and the language used was something out of a "blue-collar" bar, with profanity and shouting the normal mode of communication. For the sister and brother who took on ownership and executive management, these new roles became painful responsibilities that made them dread coming to work or having to deal with any problems in the business (an almost daily occurrence in any business). To make matters worse, both people had worked in other companies as part of their work experience, and therefore had more productive and normal environments to contrast and compare to their family-owned company.

This situation became an extremely toxic one for everyone involved. The sister and brother had to become de-sensitized to being at constant odds with all of the partners in the business. Tragically, the relationship between the sister and the brother deteriorated as well. Whereas they used to be good friends in addition to siblings, now they became estranged outside the work environment and their families ceased to have any contact with one another.

If you think this situation is unusual, think again. All you have to do is pick up a newspaper or business magazine to realize that family feuds dominate most family-owned private businesses.

Let me illustrate the family feud concept with another anecdote. This example illustrates the need for well thought out succession planning, especially in the event of death.

This family-owned business was a successful retail company that had established great success and differentiation in its market. Quite unexpectedly, as is always the case, the founder of the company died rather suddenly. He was middle-aged at the time of his death. This

144

entrepreneur had always involved his wife in the business and as a result she managed a significant piece of it. When the founder died, his will provided for his share of the business (majority shares) to be inherited by his wife. The remaining shares stayed with other members of his family.

When the founder of this retail company was alive, there was always tension and conflict amongst his family members who were involved in the business and owned some significant shares as well. While he was alive, because of the strength of his personality and his life force in establishing and growing the business, his family members were afraid of him and remained, in general, on good behavior. There were, of course, many conflicts, heated-disagreements, and abusive behavior from his extended family towards the founder and his immediate family.

Well, as you can imagine all of this toxic resentment and jealousy which was obvious, but contained while he was alive, became virulent and out of control when focused on the founder's wife, who had taken over his role in the company.

The result of all this hatred and jealousy was that the founder's wife had a very tough time managing the company since her deceased husband's family members did not recognize her authority and believed that they should be the rightful heirs to the company. As a result of the company history and family politics, the deceased husband's family decided to sue his widow for ownership of the company.

Lawyers, discoveries, legal documents, court appearances, and hundreds of thousands of dollars in legal costs have been the result of all of this. Can you imagine the on-going sorrow and anxiety the founder's wife and immediate family must have gone through? On top of all the tragedy and sadness of losing a loved one, the new female CEO still needs to carry on her husband's dream and make a living to support her children.

What could have been done differently? Probably lots of things could have been done to minimize the chances of on-going litigation and conflict between the survivors and inheritors of the founder's family.

Generally speaking, I am not in favor of extended family-owned businesses, unless the extended family has unusually strong ethics and respect for one another. Once a business starts to get quite successful and is earning millions of dollars in income, jealousy and a sense of entitlement starts to settle in. If a family is involved in the management of a company this dynamic is greatly magnified.

A lesson to be learned out of anecdotes like this is to avoid having multiple family members as owners in the company. Unless each party has brought significant capital and know-how, this is a recipe for disaster.

The other lesson learned is to have well-thought out succession plans in place in the event of a death, illness, or other unforeseen event. This succession plan should be communicated and discussed amongst all the affected parties. Much in the same way that a business develops and implements a disaster recovery plan, a succession plan should be thought of in the same vein.

Different scenarios, especially those that involve a breakdown of civility and fair-play, should be thought through, discussed, and a mitigation strategy and plan developed to address these possibilities.

No one will believe that everything will be miraculously peaceful and cooperative, but a strong succession plan will certainly minimize the opportunity for all-out World War III between family members.

Another type of family politics scenario is when you work hard to build your business, and when it takes off, you hire family members to work for you. These family members might be your husband, a parent, your children, or a sibling.

Usually having an immediate family member work in your business can be a positive experience for all, providing that each person understands his/her roles and responsibilities.

In addition, you have to understand the personality and character of people in your family. Do they have a passion for the business? Do they have unique skills that enrich the business? Do they have a strong work ethic? Do they understand that rewards are not just going to be handed to them but will have to be earned?

I have come across a couple of examples that show the potential conflict and broken relationships that can result from misalignment in expectations, values, and experience.

One such situation is a family-owned food/beverage business with an international reputation. This business owned and founded by the matriarch of the family, involved all of her children in the business. One of her children became integral in the running and growth of her business. The other children operated at satisfactory or sub-standard levels of performance, not adding tremendous value to the business.

The challenge for this mother became how she would get the non-productive children to look at working outside of the business without creating bad feelings between the siblings. In the end, things worked out for the best. The children who were non-productive employees found other careers that ultimately became more fulfilling. Unfortunately, some resentment still remained between the children, especially towards the sibling who remained in the business and played a leadership/strong-supporting role to the matriarch CEO.

Another situation involved the rapid growth of a high-tech firm led by a woman CEO. After several years of successful operation and stability, her brother expressed some interest in joining her company and becoming a sales executive. He had a great deal of relevant experience and talent but very little experience in his sister's particular industry. Both siblings agreed that it was going to be a bit of a gamble and that there would be a significant amount of training and learning involved.

After almost one year, the CEO's brother became productive and looked like he would become a valuable member of her management team, but there were cracks in their relationship after working so closely together. It was difficult for the CEO's brother to take direction from his sister, and resentment began to build within him. After offering him some shares in the company and an opportunity to continue on for another year contract, the CEO's brother decided to go on to start his own company in another field. The relationship never recovered from the brother's feelings of resentment in taking direction from his sister and his feeling that more should have been done for him. He felt that he was not compensated sufficiently and after a few disagreements with his sister felt that she should have given him more leeway from a compensation and ownership perspective.

Another potential scenario is that of a female CEO with a husband who worked alongside her in a key role. His feelings about playing a secondary role to his wife can make the difference between a successful business and marriage or dissolution of both.

A husband is definitely a unique case in the family politics scenario. Usually he becomes an equal partner in building the business, especially if he has been involved with the growth of your company from the get-go. However, if you are the CEO of the company, there is the potential for very real tension and conflict.

It takes a man with a very strong ego, not a big ego, to operate successfully within the context of a business led by his wife. If he has any self-doubt or feelings of inadequacy, such a scenario will only serve to exacerbate these negative feelings.

Let me tell you a story that will illustrate this point. A woman decided to start her own services business after many years in that particular industry. She was a star performer on all levels and had always dreamed of building her own business. She left a plum position in a large global firm to found her own company. After several years of struggling, the company finally began to take off. When it was stable and making money, her husband left an excellent job with a Fortune 50 company and joined their company in a very key role.

His role was that of a strategist, product manager, business developer, relationship manager, and consultant. Without his imagination, foresight, and creativity, the business would not have continued to grow and blossom as it did.

Yet in spite of all these tremendous accomplishments and contributions, the husband never felt that the company was equally his. He always felt a little like an interloper and under the management of his wife. These feelings occurred in spite of a very clear separation of roles and responsibilities between husband and wife. The wife made a concerted effort to stay out of his business and areas of responsibilities.

However, when it came to financial management of the company, both parties agreed that the wife was best suited to address these aspects.

Unfortunately, this husband and wife worked together very well and accomplished a great deal. The question that began to pound in both of their heads incessantly was at what cost?

There was no dividing line between work and marriage. As a result, both people felt like they worked round-the-clock because they never stopped thinking and talking about work-related maters. Because her husband felt out of control of his own destiny at times, he would focus his resentment at her in the form of constant arguments and temper tantrums over insignificant issues.

She began to feel like she was walking on egg shells and could do nothing right at work or home. He felt mounting resentment and anger at her and their business, so that the joy and passion he had initially felt in the early years of the company's development were replaced by feelings of burden and boredom.

The really tragic thing about this situation was that this couple had the power to make millions of dollars together. But as a result of misguided perceptions on both their parts and an inability to separate the relationship from their business, this couple was in danger of divorce, and the business was in danger of regression in all respects. Everything both people worked hard to achieve was potentially at risk of being lost forever.

So what did these people do? What they did was agreed to go their separate ways, business-wise but stayed together marriage-wise. The husband went off to a senior management position in a large global technology firm. The wife continued to run the business—minus the tremendous inspiration and support of her husband.

What resulted from this? Well there was a period of adjustment on all parties. It took a while for the woman to adapt to running the show, completely on her own. At times she was scared in the same way that Samson was scared when he got that bad haircut. She thought that with the absence of her husband, somehow her strength had seeped out and would never be re-captured. This was nonsense of course. She came back better and more successful than ever.

The husband went on to that dream job he had fantasized about for years. He really enjoyed the corporate perks, the atmosphere of collegial communications and relationships, the travel, and the wide variety of intellectual stimulation. In the end, his life was about experiences that he received fulfillment from. He wasn't like his wife. He didn't dream of independence and making millions and pioneering in an unknown territory. He liked the distance between them work-wise. It ultimately proved to be beneficial to their marriage. They could go back to being a couple instead of business partners.

Not all family-owned businesses experience the problems that I have described so far. Many operate quite successfully and are very supportive environments for the family members that work together.

How do you determine if your family-owned business will become a legacy that everyone can be proud of or end up in court fighting over money and ownership?

After talking and researching this issue with many family-owned companies, especially those led by a woman CEO, I have come up with a check list to help you determine whether this structure for your business will be a success or a nightmare.

Every Woman's Family Business Viability Checklist

___ Does your family have a history of successful, family-owned businesses?

___ If so, has the family flourished emotionally as well as financially?

___ Do the family members in question who will work with you in the business have excellent values and ethics?

___ Are your family members aligned with your values, ethics, and working style?

___ Do your family members take direction from you without feeling bossed around?

___ Do your family members have the required skills and experience to do the jobs they will be carrying out for you?

___ Do these particular family members like and respect one another?

___ If you are giving part ownership to your family members, have they invested the requisite amount of money to receive the appropriate level of ownership (e.g. 10% ownership means they have invested 10% of the overall value of the company)?

___ Have you written down your family member's respective roles and responsibilities and received verbal and written agreement of acceptance?

___ Have you discussed how and under what circumstances you and your family members could go their separate ways?

___ Have you discussed and agreed upon how conflict and disagreement will be resolved between you and your family members?

___ Have you documented a succession plan (documented it in a will) and communicated your wishes to all affected parties at the same time?

__ Do you and your husband have a strong and healthy marriage?

__ Are you able to separate work from family and marriage time, if you are working with your husband?

__ Does your husband have strong self esteem?

__ Does your husband have the same work/business goals as you?

__ Are you able to stick to ground rules in communication between you and your husband at work?

__ Do you enjoy working with your husband and/or other family members?

If you checked off 0-6 boxes, the chances of your family-owned business being a success are slim to none. Remember, profits at the expense of your mental and physical health will not be viable in the long-run. Feeling like you want to strangle someone the moment you get to work is not the way to promote longevity.

If you checked off 7-12 boxes, you have a 50/50 chance of building a successful family-owned business. You have observed how complex a corporate environment is. Now, magnify that complexity by a factor of 10. This factor is called the Familia effect. It basically means that when you introduce blood, egos, culture, tradition, history, and memories (not all happy ones), you are mixing a broth of potential disharmony of epic proportions. Having many positive factors is a good start for any business, but when it comes to families working together, it's anyone's guess what kind of trouble people can get themselves into.

If you checked 13-18 boxes, you have a 60-70% chance of success in building your family business and still having a happy family at the end of it all. There will still be many trials and tribulations and unforeseen maelstroms that build up from nowhere. The question is, do you have what it takes to lead a business and grow it, and on top of that manage family politics and feelings, and still be true to yourself?

That is a very tall order for anyone. It can be done and has been done by many companies all over the world. But at what price is a company built, leveraging the dynamics of family? The price is very high, and you must be prepared and ready to pay it on all accounts.

The bottom-line out of all of this discussion is, know thyself and be true to thyself! If you have that nasty disease to please you are in very big trouble. You will expend a lot of energy trying to make everyone happy and make your business a success. You may very well make your business a great success, but I guarantee that you will never make everyone happy no matter how hard you try.

The pressures and difficulties you will face in running your business will be enormous. If you have to fight battles of will and emotion with your husband, in-laws, siblings, or children, you will fail yourself. Constant emotional stress and anger is a recipe for serious health problems, not to mention an un-happy life.

In conclusion, my final word of advice is think very carefully about working with your family. Take it slowly, try introducing one family member, and see how that works. If it works well, bring on another person and try to replicate the successes you achieved with the first family member.

As you may have guessed, I am not a big fan of family-owned businesses. If you add the element of a woman CEO, I become even more concerned. I know our tendencies as women are to constantly try to please, avoid conflict, achieve peace at any cost, and put everyone ahead of ourselves. In your role as CEO, you will constantly be walking a tight rope. Adding your family to the corporate equation means that you are walking that tight rope in stilettos and blind-folded. Caveat la Familia!

CHAPTER 13
How to Sell Your Company Profitably

You are probably thinking, "Wow! This lady just started teaching us about how to get our business off the ground and now she wants to end all the fun and talk about selling it!"

Well, the purpose of this book is to walk you through everything you will need to know to start, grow, and sell your business—cradle to grave as they say.

Selling your business is going to be the most difficult thing you have done thus far. Remember, you gave birth to this business. How do you let go of it and make a truck-load of money at the same time?

I would say that you almost need to start to think about selling your business from the moment you get it started. I say this because you must consciously be attuned to how you can constantly enrich your business and create something that will hold value for many people who would consider buying it some time in the future.

Your investment and growth strategy will be predicated upon what you want your endgame to look like. There are usually five major reasons an entrepreneur decides to sell her business:

1. You want to diversify your wealth. Perhaps you believe that the market and product you are selling are on shaky ground. You may want to cash in on the returns of the business when things are still fairly rosy.

2. You might be bored and want to experience new challenges. Many entrepreneurs are motivated by the "chase," the process of building the company and seeing their ideas coming to fruition. Once the company is stable and things are humming along, you may be yearning for new challenges.

3. You want to retire. Perhaps you want to do something else altogether. You may have worked in your business for years or even decades and feel that it is time to move on to something else.

4.   Unforeseen circumstances can create the urgency to sell your business. A family illness, your own illness or death, might precipitate the need to sell your business, to allow you or your heirs to be free of their obligations to focus on other things.

5.   Someone or some other company wants to buy your business and makes you an offer you can't refuse.

Do you know that according to RSM Equico, a specialist in mergers and acquisitions, 80% of entrepreneurial sellers often leave up to 80% of the deal on the table? That is why I believe it is so important to cover some of the fundamental best practices around selling your company, so that you don't cheat yourself and your family out of everything that you are worth.

There are three reasons why companies buy other companies:

1.   Economic—this is the worst motivator for buyers because they are looking for a potential fire sale;

2.   Strategic—they see your business as being able to stretch their company's strategic reach in a particular market. This is a slightly better buying motivator than economic drivers; and

3.   Opportunistic—they see your business as delivering some unique capability they currently cannot address or achieve internally. This is one of the best drivers for buyers, as they often are willing to buy a company for a premium, if it addresses a unique opportunity.

With respect to buyers' acquisition objectives, "capturing new markets is an important motivation….M&A's are a means of achieving strategic and operational, rather than financial, corporate objectives." World Investment Report, Cross-Border Mergers and Acquisitions, United Nations.

There are a few messages I want to communicate in this section with respect to best practices for selling your company.

The first message I want to give you is start preparing to sell your company well in advance of the actual date or time frame you intend to sell. What I mean is, be aware of what is going on in your industry with respect to mergers and acquisitions. Research these types of transactions by constantly surveying newspaper and magazine article, the internet, blogs, and talking to companies that specialize in brokering sales of companies.

As you grow your business, focus on developing and enriching your core competencies or differentiators. If for example, your products are what make you unique, constantly strive to improve upon them. If your customers are your strength, ensure that you have a well-documented CRM system that captures all of your customer contact and interaction/sales information. In other words, zero in on what you consider your most important asset from a market perspective and constantly work to improve your innate strengths.

When it comes time to sell your business, give yourself plenty of lead time. You should take the time to research which service providers specialize in brokering sales of companies like yours. Interview several companies like these. Ask for references. If it is possible, speak to their references in person instead of on the phone. Many of these brokers will ask for fees up front to do the necessary financial due diligence work and a percentage of the net proceeds, once the deal is done. Be prepared to spend a significant amount of money up front for the match-making and due-diligence services.

If you do your research properly you should realize that many factors will influence the price of your company:

- Having more than one suitor, ideally three buyers will create a healthy competition for the sale of your company;
- Avoid selling your business to a buyer who is in the same business; they will be looking for a fire sale;
- Don't get sucked into the standard accounting formulas for evaluating the value of a company (e.g., companies in your industry sell for an average of 1.5 times the revenue);
- Understand your comparative value and advantage vis-à-vis the buyer and what they stand to gain from the transaction; and
- Structure a deal like you would structure a marriage; that is, try to get as much of the benefits up front and leave just a few to cash in on at the end of the transition period.

The whole point of using a match maker or acquisitions broker is that they bring several potential buyers to the table and create a competitive environment for the acquisition bid of your company. If you only have one suitor, the deal will be about how little you are willing to sell your company for, with no possibility of leveraging other bidders to drum-up your price.

If you think the best offer for your business will come from another company in your industry, think again. The research I have done, which is substantiated by an international M&A firm, RSM Equico, shows that the most lucrative deals for a seller occur when a firm outside of their industry and country purchases them. The impetus for this match might be to get access to a new market, new customers (who would probably buy the buying company's products), supply chain, technology/R&D, and/or management talent.

The kind of prospective buyer you want to go after, is a company which is big, global, public, and in a different industry than yourself, but with common potential customers. Think about it. If you are a small manufacturing company and another slightly larger manufacturer wants to buy you, do you think they will want to spend a premium to acquire you? Probably not. For one, they probably don't have the capital required, if they are slightly larger than you. In addition, they might not have the need to increase their price/earnings ratios, because they might be a privately-owned company.

The next thing you need to watch-out for is how you evaluate the value of your company. Beware of accountants and lawyers who try to use the conservative industry standards to assess the value of your company.

Some of the industry standard evaluations they typically use are multipliers of EBIT (earnings before income tax) or multipliers of EBITDA (earnings before income tax plus depreciation and amortization), which is considered to be a more accurate evaluation. EBITDA adds back amortization and depreciation, which plumps up your earnings figures. However, this is still an extremely conservative measurement, and not in your best interests as a seller.

One of the most conservative evaluation metrics is Discounted Cash Flow Valuation (DCF). This valuation is extremely disadvantageous to you the seller. The reason for this is that it is not forward looking. The DCF is based on current earnings and not on future earnings.

DCF involves a forecast of cash flows extending many years into the future and applying the time-value-of-money calculations, which discounts those cash values to their present values. DCF is a great method for a buyer to use to evaluate your company, but it is so conservative that it short changes your value.

Another method that is used to evaluate the value of a company is an asset-based approach. The asset-based approach involves equity book value, adjusted book value, liquidation value, or replacement value. There are some obvious disadvantages of this approach; one is that there is incredible intangible value a business possesses that cannot be captured in this type of evaluation.

One of the most advantageous methods of evaluation is the pro forma financial method. This involves the development of financial statements for the previous and current fiscal years, as well as a projection out to the next five years. The pro forma financial statements are done on the assumption that if there were no limitation to the investment dollars you could get your hands on, how fast and by what rate could your company grow.

Another important element of the pro forma analysis is that it translates privately owned companies' financial statements into the equivalent of publicly traded financial statements. For example, as the owner of a privately owned company, you will incur many more expenses than a publicly traded company, because your focus is on reducing your EBITA, so that you can reduce your tax liability. With the pro-forma, these expenses are added back into the income statements. As a result, a potential investor can see what your company would produce if it was not subject to the aggressive expenses/tax deductions of a private company. This method is by far the most advantageous way of measuring your company's value.

When a buyer makes an offer for your company, they typically offer some cash up front, stock options to be exercised at periodic intervals of the transition period, and a final pay out at the end of the termination period, based upon profitability of the newly acquired company.

You will be required to make a commitment to properly transition your old company to the new owners. The typical transition period averages around two years. You have to be able to stick around for the full term, so you better be sure that you can stomach taking direction from the new owners and potentially putting up with a lot of baloney, until you make your exit.

Be careful of deals that involve a small lump sum up front and a big pay out at the end of the transition. As you know, from your experience, anything can happen in a business in a two year period. If for example, the company's profitability decreases because there are a lot of new overhead costs and your pay off is predicated upon a percentage of the profits at the end of year two, you may end up with little or nothing at the end of the transition period.

Your negotiating skills will be put to the final test when you structure the sale of your company. You will have to thoroughly research your prospective buyers to understand their strengths and weaknesses and to understand the innate advantages that your company provides to the potential buyer.

No matter how sweet a deal appears to be, remember that there is always a hidden cost to pay. The transition period where you provide knowledge transfer to the buyers over a certain period of time is very much like a marriage, but with a definite expiry or divorce date. You must understand yourself and your ability to handle diversity and conflict. The buyer may purposefully make it difficult on you to stick it through, especially if the transition is not going well. So think through every possible scenario that could arise during this prolonged hand off, and create a risk mitigation strategy that addresses these potential risks.

If you decide that selling your company to an outsider is not your preferred exit strategy, there is another option. An Employment Stock Ownership Plan or ESOP, as it is commonly referred to, is a great alternate selling strategy. Let's say that you have been very successful in attracting and building a stellar management team. You could create a unique compensation perk like an ESOP. At the end of each fiscal year, when you are paying out bonuses, or profit-sharing, you can make a certain number of shares available that the employees can purchase.

An ESOP is basically a private market for which shares in the company are exchanged between the major owners and key employees for the purpose of a retirement savings plan for the employees and a means of eventually cashing out your majority shares in the company.

One very important piece of advice I would like to give to you is prepare yourself to sell your company well in advance of when you want to sell it. If your company is in a major growth period with several years of growth in revenue and profitability, you may want to accelerate your plans to sell. Remember, your company has more value and, consequently, you have more negotiating power when things are going well financially, and you are not compelled to sell. This kind of foresight is predicated upon a high degree of self awareness and knowledge. You also have to develop a bit of distance between yourself and your company so that you are not so emotionally involved and tied to it that you give up fortuitous opportunities to sell when they appear.

CHAPTER 14
Taking Care of You—
The Most Important Investment You Will Ever Make

We have covered a lot of ground so far. We have examined in detail how and what you can do to prepare the groundwork for starting a business.

We examined several major facets of executing—getting your business off the ground and growing it. Finally, we reviewed several important aspects of reaping the benefits of all of your hard work and success.

Throughout these discussions, I have tried to emphasize and weave an important theme amidst all the talk of business and money. Creating wealth is not just about dollars and cents. When someone points out a famous CEO and says that they are successful or wealthy, what does this really mean?

What does wealth mean to you? Does it mean that you have more money than you could ever know what to do with? Does it mean that at some point you will never have to work again? Does it mean that you can support as many charitable causes as you would like? Does this mean that you are famous and regularly appear in the business section of major newspapers? Does wealth mean you have a loving family and many good friends?

Wealth means different things to different people. Understanding what you want out of life, understanding yourself and what it means to be happy and healthy, and understanding your desire and responsibility to take care of your family are crucial pieces of your wealth picture.

To me, wealth is about creating a life that enriches and heals those around me. Having the financial resources to provide for my family gives me the freedom to achieve my goals.

The truth is that I can have all the financial resources in the world, all the best intentions and abilities to help and enrich others, but if I don't honor and take care of myself, all will be lost.

As a woman, a CEO, mother, wife, daughter, and friend I have had the opportunity to talk to thousands of women. The obvious theme that presents itself with all of these women is that they are the centre of a wheel with many spokes. In being the centre of so many people's lives, these women have determined that everyone else's needs must come first, before their own.

What happens when you put everyone first and yourself last? Let me describe some of the consequences of this innate female behavior.

One of the consequences of this conduct is that your health will inevitably start to suffer. Of course every woman will manifest these disturbances differently.

Some women will manifest this imbalance with weight gain (can we say emotional eating?) or loss (anorexia or bulimia). Some women will become anxious for no apparent reason, be perpetually moody, or constantly fighting PMS. Worse, many of us become depressed and don't even recognize the signs for years. Some of us will develop mysterious autoimmune diseases like irritable bowel syndrome, thyroid disorders, arthritis, and allergies, to name a small few.

Others will develop cancer, heart disease (high cholesterol, high blood pressure, diabetes are the early signs) often at the height of our careers, when we are just becoming masters of the game.

Sometimes these disturbances manifest themselves in non-health related ways like divorce, addiction, crippled relationships with loved ones, and intense loneliness and a sense of isolation.

Please don't get me wrong, I am not trying to say that putting yourself last empirically results in disease. But it certainly creates an environment, behavior, habits, and attitudes that become strong contributors to encouraging these imbalances.

I look back at my life for instance and I shake my head in wonder and disbelief at how many times I have betrayed my better self.

I came from a very happy family life with my parents and my brothers. However, my youngest brother Jimmy was born with a series of birth defects and diseases that rendered him severely mentally handicapped and with minimal kidney function. He subsequently died of kidney failure at

MOVE FROM EMPLOYEE TO CEO OF YOUR OWN DESTINY

the age of twenty-four years old. As you can imagine, the pressures and responsibilities of taking care of a special needs child laid heavily on the shoulders of my parents, and in turn on my shoulders.

From the early age of seven years old, I developed an un-naturally mature approach to life. I felt intense empathy for my parents' pain, especially my mother, and I tried very hard to support her. At the same time, I felt the need to be the best I could be to create some happiness and pride in my parents, to compensate for one of their children never leading a normal life.

This strong sense of empathy, the need to help and support those who have compromised health, a sense of strong duty to the family, and an intense desire to achieve great things to compensate for monumental sadness and disappointment became my modus operandi.

As a result of this pattern that was set since I was a child, I achieved great things in my life. But in the process of achieving and actually over achieving, I lost touch with my true self. This began to manifest in my life in interesting ways. For example, I always seemed to choose men who had "problems" that only I could fix. If my goals and work were to achieve certain financial goals, I would dramatically exceed them. I would do it in style too.

When I was pregnant with both of my children, due to my overwork and desire to overcompensate, I made my sales objectives in nine months instead of twelve, went into premature labor, and ran my consulting practice from bed where I lay for five weeks. Instead of taking the usual four months off that we were allowed by law, I took only two months and worked flex hours (including from home) for two months and received full salary and commissions during this time (instead of unemployment insurance).

Each job I took on, I did extremely well, and always tried to give a little extra. Earlier in the book, I mentioned my overachievement of all my sales and profitability objectives and then being denied a promotion. This of course served me very well in the long run, because if not for my employer's short sightedness, I would have never had the kick in the pants to start my own business.

However, there were always tell-tale signs that I would ignore. These signs would tell me that I was ignoring my needs and greatest dreams to be a good girl, I mean employee, and bring home a comfortable and secure pay-cheque. In the years before my wake-up call to start my own business, I suffered from anxiety and depression, on and off. Some of this depression could be attributed to my sense of not living my life the way I had dreamed since I was a young woman.

Some of this depression was attributed to the grief I experienced after losing all my grand parents, my brother, and my favorite aunt within a period of five years. Every time I turned around, someone I loved was dying.

On top of that, I went through some messy custody issues with my first husband that also contributed greatly to my constant anxiety for my children.

Of course, no one would ever know that I was so depressed, because I functioned at such a high-level of competence and was always smiley and upbeat at work. I was always the go-to person whenever anyone had a problem, because I knew how to listen and solve problems.

Once I began to focus on my dreams and making them a reality, I was filled with super-human strength and my depression became a vague memory. I worked my ass off for the first three years of our company's history. I literally worked triple time, or rather all the time. I was consulting on multiple engagements simultaneously and selling and marketing our company at the same time.

By the time I was thirty-five years old, I had earned more than a million dollars through our company's success. Each year after was better than the last, so that our company created a multi-million dollar net worth for our family.

But all my hard work began to take its toll and I began to face burnout, especially after those three first critical years. I was more attuned to myself by then, and as such, gave myself permission to work reduced hours and take several weeks off.

Since our company was growing every year, I thought about hiring a sales person. When my brother talked to me about how unhappy and unfulfilled he was in his job with a large Telco, I made him an offer to come and work for us.

My brother was incredibly competent, hard-working, and very intelligent. However, the information technology management consulting business was new to him, and it took him some time to learn. As with many families, the dynamics between us became strained because he didn't like taking direction from me. On my side, I was uncomfortable with pushing him too hard, for fear of upsetting him and creating a rift in our relationship. After a year, we both agreed to go our separate ways, and my brother went on to start a very successful recruiting agency.

This situation arose in large part because I had the desire to help out my brother without giving enough consideration to how we would work together. What would the impact on us and our business be?

Over that year, I began to feel constantly anxious. This should have been an important emotion that I paid attention to, but didn't. Anxiety was my body's way of telling me that this situation was not a good one for anyone—me, my brother, our families, or my business.

When my husband began to experience some serious health problems, I endeavored to take care of him and continue with my normal arduous schedule. When I began to burn the candle at both ends again, I started to notice that I was mildly depressed, and could not give myself 100% to the business, as I had done in the past.

Luckily, with some good advice from my husband and with an open mind, I agreed to hire a second-in-command for the business. This new addition to our company would help me with the sales and marketing activity, as well as manage our existing and new accounts.

Reaching out and getting more help for me in the business allowed me to maintain my health, support my husband's health issues, and continue to support the growth of our business.

Over the last few years we had many excellent people work for Knowsys. But in a few cases, my need to fix things and empathize with people's personal challenges resulted in me creating a work environment where people felt that they would be given extra time to correct deficiencies in their performance. I have to say that this approach worked very well in several cases, in that those employees turned things around quite well. But in other cases, people abused my good will and took obvious advantage of the situation.

Again, my body would tell me that something was wrong with strong feelings of anxiety, anger, daily hives, and constant fatigue. But sometimes I would wait too long, until I was at the boiling point and then make the decision to fire someone when it should have been done weeks, if not months, before.

The reason I described some of my personal and business history is that many of you will see similarities with your own experiences. Just because you gain success and financial wealth doesn't mean that you don't have to deal with your share of periodic annihilation. In overcoming major hurdles, conflicts, and obstacles, we develop almost super-human strengths. We also experience the impact of these challenges, as I mentioned earlier, in the form of health or emotional problems.

So, how should you take care of yourself, since you are your most valuable investment? The answers are not always easy. But if you live through enough crises and melodrama, and suffer health, family, or emotional problems, you learn some important lessons.

The first lesson is to know yourself and understand what your core, non-negotiable values are. This is a hole we often fall into, especially when money and success are involved. Remember if you contradict your core values, you might make a lot of money, but you will pay a heavy price in so many other ways. For example, your body will often send you signals that something isn't right. You can choose to ignore these signals, but they will just get that much more insistent and louder, until you can choose to ignore them no longer.

If your business and life are out of synch with whom you are, something will have to give. Either you will sabotage yourself or you might not be able to maintain and grow from your initial success.

Make sure your business is a reflection of your highest self and that the values and way you and your employees conduct themselves is a reflection of the values you hold most dear.

The second lesson is to maximize your health and joy factor. You can only do this by taking care of yourself and giving yourself permission to relax and have fun.

By maximizing your health, I mean, taking the time:
- to spend quality and quantity fun time with your loved ones;
- to interact with friends socially, on a regular basis;
- to go to regular doctor's and dental check-ups;
- to eat for nourishment and fuel, not just for weight loss or as an after-thought;
- for regular, consistent exercise at least one hour per day, six days per week (at least two hours of the six should involve weight training as this preserves bone density and muscle as we age);

- for regular vacations, even if it is just a long—weekend every month or two;
- to meditate or pray on a daily basis, even if it is just for a few minutes;
- to cultivate hobbies and interests like playing music or learning a new language; and
- to learn and get new work/professional knowledge, skills, and professional designations.

The third lesson is to learn to ask for help when you feel overwhelmed or you feel that you are not able to handle your load. Be an expert at delegating tasks to others. My mantra has become, when in doubt—delegate. Of course, this is very hard to do when you are an over-functioning super-hero. But try it once and then practice delegating at least three tasks a week. Within a month, you will be delegating any task that can be done by anyone else, as well as you do it. The result will be a lighter step and more of your time being spent on tasks that only you can bring your unique talents to.

Remember the old anti-drugs campaign, with its signature statement of "just say no"? Well, let this be the message of lesson number four. Yes, I know it is killing you to say it, but just try. Cure yourself of the disease to please and learn to say no. The world will not fall apart. People will still like and respect you. Saying no will not change that if they are your true friends. This behavior is probably one of the most important habits you need to develop if you want to maximize your business productivity and personal joy quotient.

Your fifth lesson is to love yourself. Revel in your own glory. Be happy with what you have achieved and know that you are doing the best you can do. Yes, we over achievers are naturally never happy with where we are, we always want to go further. That is fine. It is ok to always want to improve and grow.

But the bottom line is, cherish yourself. You have to know unequivocally how special you are. When you truly love yourself and appreciate your unique strengths, you will operate in "the groove," in all aspects of your life. When you face life's challenges from a position of self-esteem, you will always make the right decisions.

The last lesson in taking the best care of you is to differentiate between yourself and your business achievements.

Remember, you are not your business. You are not your profession. You are not your wealth. Many people confuse what they do with who they are. Until you understand this irrefutable reality, you will always tie your happiness to external influences.

Consequently, you will always feel dissatisfied with yourself if you are not constantly achieving the un-achievable. When you truly accept that you have value just because of who you are, then you can approach the road ahead with a sense of direction, a clearly marked map, and an unquestionable faith in your humanity.

BIBLIOGRAPHY AND RECOMMENDED READING LIST

Pat and Ruth Williams, How to be Like Women of Influence—Life Lessons from 20 of the Greatest, Health Communications Inc.

Entrepreneur's Toolkit, Tools and Techniques to Launch and Grow Your Business, 2005 Harvard Business School Publishing Corporation.

Stephen E. Heiman, Diane Sanchez, The New Strategic Selling, 1998, Warner Books.

Harvard Business Review on Finding and Keeping the Best People, 1994, Harvard Business School Publishing Corporation.

Rudolph W. Giuliani, Leadership, 2002, Hyperion Publishing

Juan Enriquez, As the Future Catches You, 2000 Crown Publishing Group.

Marshall Goldsmith, Laurence Lyons, Alyssa Freas, Coaching for Leadership, How the World's Greatest Coaches Help Leaders Learn, 2000, Jossey-Bass/Pfeiffer.

Richard Carlson, Don't Sweat the Small Stuff and it's all small stuff, 1997, Hyperion Publishing.

Richard Carlson, What About the Big Stuff? Finding Strength and Moving Forward When the Stakes Are High, 2002 Hyperion Publishing.

Martha Stewart, The Martha Rules, 2005, Martha Stewart Living Omnimedia, Inc.

Thomas L. Harrison, Instinct, Tapping Your Entrepreneurial DNA to Achieve Your Business Goals, 2005, Time Warner Group.

Jack Canfield, The Success Principles, 2005, HarperCollins Publishers, Inc.

SARK, Make your Creative Dreams Real, 2004, Simon and Schuster.

Anthony Robbins, Awaken the Giant Within, 1991 Free Press (A Division of Simon and Schuster).

Tama J. Kieves, This Time I Dance! Trusting the Journey of Creating the Work You Love, 2002 Awakening Artistry Press.

Deepak Chopra, The Spontaneous Fulfillment of Desire, 2003 Harmony Books.

Tobin Blake, The Power of Stillness-Learn Meditation in 30 Days, 2003 New World Library.

RSM Equico, Mergers and Acquisitions Course.